INTERM...

MYTHOLOGIES

Roland Barthes was born in 1915 and studied French
literature and classics at the University of Paris. After
teaching French at universities in Rumania and Egypt,
he joined the Centre National de Recherche Scientifique,
where he devoted himself to research in sociology and
lexicology. He was a professor at the Collège de France
until his death in 1980.

7

ALSO AVAILABLE IN VINTAGE

A Barthes Reader
(with an introduction by Susan Sontag)
Camera Lucida

Roland Barthes

MYTHOLOGIES

SELECTED AND TRANSLATED FROM
THE FRENCH BY
Annette Lavers

V

VINTAGE

First published in Vintage 1993

2 4 6 8 10 9 7 5 3

Selected and translated from the French *Mythologies*
© 1957 by Editions du Seuil, Paris
Translation © 1972 by Jonathan Cape Ltd

Of the essays reproduced in this book, 'The World of Wrestling'
first appeared in *Esprit*, 'The Writer on Holiday'
in *France-Observateur*, and the remainder in *Les Lettres Nouvelles*

First published in Great Britain by Jonathan Cape Ltd, 1972

Vintage Books
Random House UK Ltd, 20 Vauxhall Bridge Road, London SW1V 2SA

Random House Australia (Pty) Limited
20 Alfred Street, Milsons Point, Sydney,
New South Wales 2061, Australia

Random House New Zealand Limited
18 Poland Road, Glenfield
Auckland 10, New Zealand

Random House South Africa (Pty) Limited
PO Box 337, Bergvlei, South Africa

Random House UK Limited Reg. No. 954009

A CIP catalogue record for this book
is available from the British Library

ISBN 0 09 997220 4

Printed and bound in Great Britain by
Cox & Wyman Ltd, Reading, Berkshire

Contents

CONTENTS

Translator's Note

The style of *Mythologies*, which strikes one at first as being highly poetic and idiosyncratic, later reveals a quasi-technical use of certain terms. This is in part due to an effort to account for the phenomena of mass culture by resorting to new models.

First and foremost among such models, as indicated in the Preface, is linguistics, whose mark is seen not so much in the use of a specialized vocabulary as in the extension to other fields of words normally reserved for speech or writing, such as *transcription*, *retort*, *reading*, *univocal* (all used in connection with wrestling), or *to decipher* (plastics or the 'good French Wine'). The author's teaching is also associated with a rediscovery of ancient rhetoric, which provides one of the connotations of the word *figure* when it is used in connection with cooking or wrestling.

Spectacle and *gesture* are often irreplaceable and refer to the interplay of action, representation and alienation in man and in society. Other terms belong to philosophical vocabulary, whether traditional (e.g. *substance*, which also has echoes of Bachelard and Hjelmslev), Sartrean/Marxist (e.g. a paradox, a car or a cathedral are said to be *consumed* by the public), or recent (e.g. *closure*, which heralds the combinative approach of semiology and its philosophical consequences). *Transference* connotes the discoveries of psycho-analysis on the relations between the abstract and the concrete. There is in addition a somewhat humorous plea for a reasoned use of neologism (cf. pp. 120-21) which foreshadows later reflections on the mutual support of linguistic and social conventions.

Such characteristics have been kept in the hope of retaining some of the flavour of the original.

Finally, the author's footnotes are indicated by numerals, and the translator's by asterisks.

Preface to the 1970 edition
(Collection 'Points', Le Seuil, Paris)

This book has a double theoretical framework: on the one hand, an ideological critique bearing on the language of so-called mass-culture; on the other, a first attempt to analyse semiologically the mechanics of this language. I had just read Saussure and as a result acquired the conviction that by treating 'collective representations' as sign-systems, one might hope to go further than the pious show of unmasking them and account *in detail* for the mystification which transforms petit-bourgeois culture into a universal nature.

It is obvious that the two attitudes which determined the origin of the book could no longer today be maintained unchanged (this is why I have made no attempt to bring it up to date). Not because what brought them about has now disappeared, but because ideological criticism, at the very moment when the need for it was again made brutally evident (May '68), has become more sophisticated, or at least ought to do so. Moreover semiological analysis, initiated, at least as far as I am concerned, in the final essay of *Mythologies*, has developed, become more precise, complicated and differentiated: it has become the theoretical locus wherein a certain liberation of 'the significant', in our country and in the West, may well be enacted. I could not therefore write a new series of mythologies in the form presented here, which belongs to the past.

What remains, however, beside the essential enemy (the bourgeois norm), is the necessary conjunction of these two enterprises: no denunciation without an appropriate method of detailed analysis, no semiology which cannot, in the last analysis, be acknowledged as *semioclasm*.*

February 1970   R. B.

* See Translator's Note on neologism.

Preface

The following essays were written one each month for about two years, from 1954 to 1956, on topics suggested by current events. I was at the time trying to reflect regularly on some myths of French daily life. The media which prompted these reflections may well appear heterogeneous (a newspaper article, a photograph in a weekly, a film, a show, an exhibition), and their subject-matter very arbitrary: I was of course guided by my own current interests.

The starting point of these reflections was usually a feeling of impatience at the sight of the 'naturalness' with which newspapers, art and common sense constantly dress up a reality which, even though it is the one we live in, is undoubtedly determined by history. In short, in the account given of our contemporary circumstances, I resented seeing Nature and History confused at every turn, and I wanted to track down, in the decorative display of *what-goes-without-saying*, the ideological abuse which, in my view, is hidden there.

Right from the start, the notion of myth seemed to me to explain these examples of the falsely obvious. At that time, I still used the word 'myth' in its traditional sense. But I was already certain of a fact from which I later tried to draw all the consequences: myth is a language. So that while concerning myself with phenomena apparently most unlike literature (a wrestling-match, an elaborate dish, a plastics exhibition), I did not feel I was leaving the field of this general semiology of our bourgeois world, the literary aspect of which I had begun to study in earlier essays. It was only, however, after having explored a number of current social phenomena that I attempted to define contemporary myth in methodical fashion; I have naturally placed this particular essay at the end of the book, since all it does is systematize topics discussed previously.

Having been written month by month, these essays do not

pretend to show any organic development: the link between them is rather one of insistence and repetition. For while I don't know whether, as the saying goes, 'things which are repeated are pleasing',* my belief is that they are significant. And what I sought throughout this book were significant features. Is this a significance which *I* read into them? In other words, is there a mythology of the mythologist? No doubt, and the reader will easily see where I stand. But to tell the truth, I don't think that this is quite the right way of stating the problem. 'De-mystification'—to use a word which is beginning to show signs of wear—is not an Olympian operation. What I mean is that I cannot countenance the traditional belief which postulates a natural dichotomy between the objectivity of the scientist and the subjectivity of the writer, as if the former were endowed with a 'freedom' and the latter with a 'vocation' equally suitable for spiriting away or sublimating the actual limitations of their situation. What I claim is to live to the full the contradiction of my time, which may well make sarcasm the condition of truth.

1957   R. B.

* 'Bis repetita placent': a paraphrase, used in French, of Horace's saying 'Haec decies repetita placebit' (*Ars Poetica*).

MYTHOLOGIES

The World of Wrestling

> The grandiloquent truth of gestures
> on life's great occasions.
>
> Baudelaire

The virtue of all-in wrestling is that it is the spectacle of excess.
Here we find a grandiloquence which must have been that of
ancient theatres. And in fact wrestling is an open-air spectacle,
for what makes the circus or the arena what they are is not the
sky (a romantic value suited rather to fashionable occasions), it is
the drenching and vertical quality of the flood of light. Even
hidden in the most squalid Parisian halls, wrestling partakes of
the nature of the great solar spectacles, Greek drama and bull-
fights: in both, a light without shadow generates an emotion
without reserve.

There are people who think that wrestling is an ignoble sport.
Wrestling is not a sport, it is a spectacle, and it is no more
ignoble to attend a wrestled performance of Suffering than a
performance of the sorrows of Arnolphe or Andromaque.* Of
course, there exists a false wrestling, in which the participants
unnecessarily go to great lengths to make a show of a fair fight;
this is of no interest. True wrestling, wrongly called amateur
wrestling, is performed in second-rate halls, where the public
spontaneously attunes itself to the spectacular nature of the
contest, like the audience at a suburban cinema. Then these same
people wax indignant because wrestling is a stage-managed sport
(which ought, by the way, to mitigate its ignominy). The public is
completely uninterested in knowing whether the contest is
rigged or not, and rightly so; it abandons itself to the primary
virtue of the spectacle, which is to abolish all motives and all
consequences: what matters is not what it thinks but what it
sees.

This public knows very well the distinction between wrestling
and boxing; it knows that boxing is a Jansenist sport, based on a
demonstration of excellence. One can bet on the outcome of a

* In Molière's *L'École des Femmes* and Racine's *Andromaque*.

15

boxing-match: with wrestling, it would make no sense. A boxing-match is a story which is constructed before the eyes of the spectator; in wrestling, on the contrary, it is each moment which is intelligible, not the passage of time. The spectator is not interested in the rise and fall of fortunes; he expects the transient image of certain passions. Wrestling therefore demands an immediate reading of the juxtaposed meanings, so that there is no need to connect them. The logical conclusion of the contest does not interest the wrestling-fan, while on the contrary a boxing-match always implies a science of the future. In other words, wrestling is a sum of spectacles, of which no single one is a function: each moment imposes the total knowledge of a passion which rises erect and alone, without ever extending to the crowning moment of a result.

Thus the function of the wrestler is not to win; it is to go exactly through the motions which are expected of him. It is said that judo contains a hidden symbolic aspect; even in the midst of efficiency, its gestures are measured, precise but restricted, drawn accurately but by a stroke without volume. Wrestling, on the contrary, offers excessive gestures, exploited to the limit of their meaning. In judo, a man who is down is hardly down at all, he rolls over, he draws back, he eludes defeat, or, if the latter is obvious, he immediately disappears; in wrestling, a man who is down is exaggeratedly so, and completely fills the eyes of the spectators with the intolerable spectacle of his powerlessness.

This function of grandiloquence is indeed the same as that of ancient theatre, whose principle, language and props (masks and buskins) concurred in the exaggeratedly visible explanation of a Necessity. The gesture of the vanquished wrestler signifying to the world a defeat which, far from disguising, he emphasizes and holds like a pause in music, corresponds to the mask of antiquity meant to signify the tragic mode of the spectacle. In wrestling, as on the stage in antiquity, one is not ashamed of one's suffering, one knows how to cry, one has a liking for tears.

Each sign in wrestling is therefore endowed with an absolute clarity, since one must always understand everything on the spot. As soon as the adversaries are in the ring, the public is overwhelmed with the obviousness of the roles. As in the theatre, each physical type expresses to excess the part which has been assigned to the contestant. Thauvin, a fifty-year-old with an obese and sagging body, whose type of asexual hideousness always inspires feminine nicknames, displays in his flesh the characters of baseness, for his part is to represent what, in the classical concept of the *salaud*, the 'bastard' (the key-concept of any wrestling-match), appears as organically repugnant. The nausea voluntarily provoked by Thauvin shows therefore a very extended use of signs: not only is ugliness used here in order to signify baseness, but in addition ugliness is wholly gathered into a particularly repulsive quality of matter: the pallid collapse of dead flesh (the public calls Thauvin *la barbaque*, 'stinking meat'), so that the passionate condemnation of the crowd no longer stems from its judgment, but instead from the very depth of its humours. It will thereafter let itself be frenetically embroiled in an idea of Thauvin which will conform entirely with this physical origin: his actions will perfectly correspond to the essential viscosity of his personage.

It is therefore in the body of the wrestler that we find the first key to the contest. I know from the start that all of Thauvin's actions, his treacheries, cruelties and acts of cowardice, will not fail to measure up to the first image of ignobility he gave me; I can trust him to carry out intelligently and to the last detail all the gestures of a kind of amorphous baseness, and thus fill to the brim the image of the most repugnant bastard there is: the bastard-octopus. Wrestlers therefore have a physique as peremptory as those of the characters of the *Commedia dell'Arte*, who display in advance, in their costumes and attitudes, the future contents of their parts: just as Pantaloon can never be anything but a ridiculous cuckold, Harlequin an astute servant and the Doctor a stupid pedant, in the same way Thauvin will never be anything but an ignoble traitor, Reinières (a tall blond fellow with a limp body and unkempt hair) the moving image of passivity, Mazaud (short and arrogant like a cock) that of grotesque conceit, and Orsano (an effeminate teddy-boy first seen in a blue-and-pink dressing-gown) that, doubly humorous, of a vindictive *salope*, or bitch (for I do not think that the public of the Elysée-Montmartre, like Littré, believes the word *salope* to be a masculine).

The physique of the wrestlers therefore constitutes a basic sign, which like a seed contains the whole fight. But this seed proliferates, for it is at every turn during the fight, in each new situation, that the body of the wrestler casts to the public the magical entertainment of a temperament which finds its natural expression in a gesture. The different strata of meaning throw light on each other, and form the most intelligible of spectacles. Wrestling is like a diacritic writing: above the fundamental meaning of his body, the wrestler arranges comments which are episodic but always opportune, and constantly help the reading of the fight by means of gestures, attitudes and mimicry which make the intention utterly obvious. Sometimes the wrestler triumphs with a repulsive sneer while kneeling on the good sportsman; sometimes he gives the crowd a conceited smile which forebodes an early revenge; sometimes, pinned to the ground, he hits the floor ostentatiously to make evident to all the intolerable nature of his situation; and sometimes he erects a complicated set of signs meant to make the public understand that he legitimately personifies the ever-entertaining image of the grumbler, endlessly confabulating about his displeasure.

We are therefore dealing with a real Human Comedy, where the most socially-inspired nuances of passion (conceit, rightfulness, refined cruelty, a sense of 'paying one's debts') always felicitously find the clearest sign which can receive them, express them and triumphantly carry them to the confines of the hall. It is obvious that at such a pitch, it no longer matters whether the passion is genuine or not. What the public wants is the image of passion, not passion itself. There is no more a problem of truth in wrestling than in the theatre. In both, what is expected is the intelligible representation of moral situations which are usually private. This emptying out of interiority to the benefit of its exterior signs, this exhaustion of the content by the form, is the very principle of triumphant classical art. Wrestling is an immediate pantomime, infinitely more efficient than the dramatic pantomime, for the wrestler's gesture needs no anecdote, no decor, in short no transference in order to appear true.

Each moment in wrestling is therefore like an algebra which instantaneously unveils the relationship between a cause and its represented effect. Wrestling fans certainly experience a kind of intellectual pleasure in *seeing* the moral mechanism function so perfectly. Some wrestlers, who are great comedians, entertain as much as a Molière character, because they succeed in imposing an immediate reading of their inner nature: Armand Mazaud, a wrestler of an arrogant and ridiculous character (as one says that Harpagon* is a character), always delights the audience by the mathematical rigour of his transcriptions, carrying the form of his gestures to the furthest reaches of their meaning, and giving to his manner of fighting the kind of vehemence and precision found in a great scholastic disputation, in which what is at stake is at once the triumph of pride and the formal concern with truth.

What is thus displayed for the public is the great spectacle of Suffering, Defeat, and Justice. Wrestling presents man's suffering with all the amplification of tragic masks. The wrestler who suffers in a hold which is reputedly cruel (an arm-lock, a twisted leg) offers an excessive portrayal of Suffering; like a primitive Pietà, he exhibits for all to see his face, exaggeratedly contorted by an intolerable affliction. It is obvious, of course, that in wrestling reserve would be out of place, since it is opposed to the voluntary ostentation of the spectacle, to this Exhibition of Suffering which is the very aim of the fight. This is why all the actions which produce suffering are particularly spectacular, like the gesture of a conjuror who holds out his cards clearly to the public. Suffering which appeared without intelligible cause would not be understood; a concealed action that was actually cruel would transgress the unwritten rules of wrestling and would have no more sociological efficacy than a mad or parasitic gesture. On the contrary suffering appears as inflicted with emphasis and conviction, for everyone must not only see that the

* In Molière's *L'Avare*.

man suffers, but also and above all understand why he suffers. What wrestlers call a hold, that is, any figure which allows one to immobilize the adversary indefinitely and to have him at one's mercy, has precisely the function of preparing in a conventional, therefore intelligible, fashion the spectacle of suffering, of methodically establishing the conditions of suffering. The inertia of the vanquished allows the (temporary) victor to settle in his cruelty and to convey to the public this terrifying slowness of the torturer who is certain about the outcome of his actions; to grind the face of one's powerless adversary or to scrape his spine with one's fist with a deep and regular movement, or at least to produce the superficial appearance of such gestures: wrestling is the only sport which gives such an externalized image of torture. But here again, only the image is involved in the game, and the spectator does not wish for the actual suffering of the contestant; he only enjoys the perfection of an iconography. It is not true that wrestling is a sadistic spectacle: it is only an intelligible spectacle.

There is another figure, more spectacular still than a hold; it is the forearm smash, this loud slap of the forearm, this embryonic punch with which one clouts the chest of one's adversary, and which is accompanied by a dull noise and the exaggerated sagging of a vanquished body. In the forearm smash, catastrophe is brought to the point of maximum obviousness, so much so that ultimately the gesture appears as no more than a symbol; this is going too far, this is transgressing the moral rules of wrestling, where all signs must be excessively clear, but must not let the intention of clarity be seen. The public then shouts 'He's laying it on!', not because it regrets the absence of real suffering, but because it condemns artifice: as in the theatre, one fails to put the part across as much by an excess of sincerity as by an excess of formalism.

We have already seen to what extent wrestlers exploit the resources of a given physical style, developed and put to use in order to unfold before the eyes of the public a total image of Defeat. The flaccidity of tall white bodies which collapse with one blow or crash into the ropes with arms flailing, the inertia of

THE WORLD OF WRESTLING

massive wrestlers rebounding pitiably off all the elastic surfaces of the ring, nothing can signify more clearly and more passionately the exemplary abasement of the vanquished. Deprived of all resilience, the wrestler's flesh is no longer anything but an un-speakable heap spread out on the floor, where it solicits relentless reviling and jubilation. There is here a paroxysm of meaning in the style of antiquity, which can only recall the heavily under-lined intentions in Roman triumphs. At other times, there is another ancient posture which appears in the coupling of the wrestlers, that of the suppliant who, at the mercy of his opponent, on bended knees, his arms raised above his head, is slowly brought down by the vertical pressure of the victor. In wrestling, unlike judo, Defeat is not a conventional sign, abandoned as soon as it is understood; it is not an outcome, but quite the contrary, it is a duration, a display, it takes up the ancient myths of public Suffering and Humiliation: the cross and the pillory. It is as if the wrestler is crucified in broad daylight and in the sight of all. I have heard it said of a wrestler stretched on the ground: 'He is dead, little Jesus, there, on the cross,' and these ironic words revealed the hidden roots of a spectacle which enacts the exact gestures of the most ancient purifications.

But what wrestling is above all meant to portray is a purely moral concept: that of justice. The idea of 'paying' is essential to wrestling, and the crowd's 'Give it to him' means above all else 'Make him pay'. This is therefore, needless to say, an immanent justice. The baser the action of the 'bastard', the more delighted the public is by the blow which he justly receives in return. If the villain—who is of course a coward—takes refuge behind the ropes, claiming unfairly to have a right to do so by a brazen mimicry, he is inexorably pursued there and caught, and the crowd is jubilant at seeing the rules broken for the sake of a deserved punishment. Wrestlers know very well how to play up to the capacity for indignation of the public by presenting the very limit of the concept of Justice, this outermost zone of confrontation where it is enough to infringe the rules a little more to open the gates of a world without restraints. For a wrestling-fan, nothing is finer than the revengeful fury of a

betrayed fighter who throws himself vehemently not on a successful opponent but on the smarting image of foul play. Naturally,
it is the pattern of Justice which matters here, much more than its
content: wrestling is above all a quantitative sequence of compensations (an eye for an eye, a tooth for a tooth). This explains
why sudden changes of circumstances have in the eyes of
wrestling habitués a sort of moral beauty: they enjoy them as they
would enjoy an inspired episode in a novel, and the greater the
contrast between the success of a move and the reversal of
fortune, the nearer the good luck of a contestant to his downfall,
the more satisfying the dramatic mime is felt to be. Justice is
therefore the embodiment of a possible transgression; it is from
the fact that there is a Law that the spectacle of the passions
which infringe it derives its value.

It is therefore easy to understand why out of five wrestling-
matches, only about one is fair. One must realize, let it be
repeated, that 'fairness' here is a role or a genre, as in the theatre:
the rules do not at all constitute a real constraint; they are the
conventional appearance of fairness. So that in actual fact a fair
fight is nothing but an exaggeratedly polite one: the contestants
confront each other with zeal, not rage; they can remain in
control of their passions, they do not punish their beaten
opponent relentlessly, they stop fighting as soon as they are
ordered to do so, and congratulate each other at the end of a
particularly arduous episode, during which, however, they have
not ceased to be fair. One must of course understand here that all
these polite actions are brought to the notice of the public by the
most conventional gestures of fairness: shaking hands, raising
the arms, ostensibly avoiding a fruitless hold which would detract
from the perfection of the contest.

Conversely, foul play exists only in its excessive signs:
administering a big kick to one's beaten opponent, taking refuge
behind the ropes while ostensibly invoking a purely formal right,
refusing to shake hands with one's opponent before or after
the fight, taking advantage of the end of the round to rush
treacherously at the adversary from behind, fouling him while the
referee is not looking (a move which obviously only has any value

or function because in fact half the audience can see it and get indignant about it). Since Evil is the natural climate of wrestling, a fair fight has chiefly the value of being an exception. It surprises the aficionado, who greets it when he sees it as an anachronism and a rather sentimental throwback to the sporting tradition ('Aren't they playing fair, those two'); he feels suddenly moved at the sight of the general kindness of the world, but would probably die of boredom and indifference if wrestlers did not quickly return to the orgy of evil which alone makes good wrestling.

Extrapolated, fair wrestling could lead only to boxing or judo, whereas true wrestling derives its originality from all the excesses which make it a spectacle and not a sport. The ending of a boxing-match or a judo-contest is abrupt, like the full-stop which closes a demonstration. The rhythm of wrestling is quite different, for its natural meaning is that of rhetorical amplification: the emotional magniloquence, the repeated paroxysms, the exasperation of the retorts can only find their natural outcome in the most baroque confusion. Some fights, among the most successful kind, are crowned by a final charivari, a sort of unrestrained fantasia where the rules, the laws of the genre, the referee's censuring and the limits of the ring are abolished, swept away by a triumphant disorder which overflows into the hall and carries off pell-mell wrestlers, seconds, referee and spectators.

It has already been noted that in America wrestling represents a sort of mythological fight between Good and Evil (of a quasi-political nature, the 'bad' wrestler always being supposed to be a Red). The process of creating heroes in French wrestling is very different, being based on ethics and not on politics. What the public is looking for here is the gradual construction of a highly moral image: that of the perfect 'bastard'. One comes to wrestling in order to attend the continuing adventures of a single major leading character, permanent and multiform like Punch or Scapino, inventive in unexpected figures and yet always faithful to his role. The 'bastard' is here revealed as a Molière character or a 'portrait' by La Bruyère, that is to say as a classical entity, an essence, whose acts are only significant epiphenomena arranged in time. This stylized character does not belong to any particular nation or party, and whether the wrestler is called Kuzchenko (nicknamed Moustache after Stalin), Yerpazian, Gaspardi, Jo Vignola or Nollières, the aficionado does not attribute to him any country except 'fairness' — observing the rules.

What then is a 'bastard' for this audience composed in part, we are told, of people who are themselves outside the rules of society? Essentially someone unstable, who accepts the rules only when they are useful to him and transgresses the formal continuity of attitudes. He is unpredictable, therefore asocial. He takes refuge behind the law when he considers that it is in his favour, and breaks it when he finds it useful to do so. Sometimes he rejects the formal boundaries of the ring and goes on hitting an adversary legally protected by the ropes, sometimes he re-establishes these boundaries and claims the protection of what he did not respect a few minutes earlier. This inconsistency, far more than treachery or cruelty, sends the audience beside itself with rage: offended not in its morality but in its logic, it considers the contradiction of arguments as the basest of crimes. The forbidden move becomes dirty only when it destroys a quantitative equilibrium and disturbs the rigorous reckoning of compensations; what is condemned by the audience is not at all the transgression of insipid official rules, it is the lack of revenge, the absence of a punishment. So that there is nothing more exciting for a crowd than the grandiloquent kick given to a vanquished 'bastard'; the joy of punishing is at its climax when it is supported by a mathematical justification; contempt is then unrestrained. One is no longer dealing with a *salaud* but with a *salope* — the verbal gesture of the ultimate degradation.

Such a precise finality demands that wrestling should be exactly what the public expects of it. Wrestlers, who are very experienced, know perfectly how to direct the spontaneous episodes of the fight so as to make them conform to the image which the public has of the great legendary themes of its mythology. A wrestler can irritate or disgust, he never disappoints, for he always accomplishes completely, by a progressive solidification of signs, what the public expects of him. In wrestling, nothing exists except in the absolute, there is no symbol, no allusion, everything is presented exhaustively. Leaving nothing in the shade, each action discards all parasitic meanings and ceremonially offers to the public a pure and full signification, rounded like Nature. This grandiloquence is nothing but the popular and age-old image of the perfect intelligibility of reality. What is portrayed by wrestling is therefore an ideal understanding of things; it is the euphoria of men raised for a while above the constitutive ambiguity of everyday situations and placed before the panoramic view of a univocal Nature, in which signs at last correspond to causes, without obstacle, without evasion, without contradiction.

When the hero or the villain of the drama, the man who was seen a few minutes earlier possessed by moral rage, magnified into a sort of metaphysical sign, leaves the wrestling hall, impassive, anonymous, carrying a small suitcase and arm-in-arm with his wife, no one can doubt that wrestling holds that power of transmutation which is common to the Spectacle and to Religious Worship. In the ring, and even in the depths of their voluntary ignominy, wrestlers remain gods because they are, for a few moments, the key which opens Nature, the pure gesture which separates Good from Evil, and unveils the form of a Justice which is at last intelligible.

The Romans in Films

In Mankiewicz's *Julius Caesar*, all the characters are wearing fringes. Some have them curly, some straggly, some tufted, some oily, all have them well combed, and the bald are not admitted, although there are plenty to be found in Roman history. Those who have little hair have not been let off for all that, and the hairdresser—the king-pin of the film—has still managed to produce one last lock which duly reaches the top of the forehead, one of those Roman foreheads, whose smallness has at all times indicated a specific mixture of self-righteousness, virtue and conquest.

What then is associated with these insistent fringes? Quite simply the label of Roman-ness. We therefore see here the main-spring of the Spectacle—the *sign*—operating in the open. The frontal lock overwhelms one with evidence, no one can doubt that he is in Ancient Rome. And this certainty is permanent: the actors speak, act, torment themselves, debate 'questions of universal import', without losing, thanks to this little flag displayed on their foreheads, any of their historical plausibility. Their general representativeness can even expand in complete safety, cross the ocean and the centuries, and merge into the Yankee mugs of Hollywood extras: no matter, everyone is reassured, installed in the quiet certainty of a universe without duplicity, where Romans are Romans thanks to the most legible of signs: hair on the forehead.

A Frenchman, to whose eyes American faces still have something exotic, finds comical the combination of the morphologies of these gangster-sheriffs with the little Roman fringe: it rather looks like an excellent music-hall gag. This is because for the French the sign in this case overshoots the target and discredits itself by letting its aim appear clearly. But this very fringe, when combed on the only naturally Latin forehead in the film, that of Marlon Brando, impresses us and does not make us laugh; and it is not impossible that part of the success of this actor in Europe is due to the perfect integration of Roman capillary habits with the general morphology of the characters he usually portrays. Conversely, one cannot believe in Julius Caesar, whose physiognomy is that of an Anglo-Saxon lawyer—a face with which one is already acquainted through a thousand bit parts in thrillers or comedies, and a compliant skull on which the hairdresser has raked, with great effort, a lock of hair.

In the category of capillary meanings, here is a sub-sign, that of nocturnal surprises: Portia and Calpurnia, woken up at dead of night, have conspicuously uncombed hair. The former, who is young, expresses disorder by flowing locks: her unreadiness is, so to speak, of the first degree. The latter, who is middle-aged, exhibits a more painstaking vulnerability: a plait winds round her neck and comes to rest on her right shoulder so as to impose the traditional sign of disorder, asymmetry. But these signs are at the same time excessive and ineffectual: they postulate a 'nature' which they have not even the courage to acknowledge fully: they are not 'fair and square'.

Yet another sign in this *Julius Caesar*: all the faces sweat constantly. Labourers, soldiers, conspirators, all have their austere and tense features streaming (with Vaseline). And close-ups are so frequent that evidently sweat here is an attribute with a purpose. Like the Roman fringe or the nocturnal plait, sweat is a sign. Of what? Of moral feeling. Everyone is sweating because everyone is debating something within himself; we are here supposed to be in the locus of a horribly tormented virtue, that is, in the very locus of tragedy, and it is sweat which has the function of conveying this. The populace, upset by the death of Caesar, then by the arguments of Mark Antony, is sweating, and com- bining economically, in this single sign, the intensity of its emotion and the simplicity of its condition. And the virtuous men, Brutus, Cassius, Casca, are ceaselessly perspiring too, testifying thereby to the enormous physiological labour produced in them by a virtue just about to give birth to a crime. To sweat is to think—which evidently rests on the postulate, appropriate to a nation of businessmen, that thought is a violent, cataclysmic operation, of which sweat is only the most benign symptom. In the whole film, there is but one man who does not sweat and who remains smooth-faced, unperturbed and water-tight: Caesar. Of course Caesar, the *object* of the crime, remains dry since *he* does not know, *he does not think*, and so must keep the firm and polished texture of an exhibit standing isolated in the courtroom.

Here again, the sign is ambiguous: it remains on the surface, yet does not for all that give up the attempt to pass itself off as depth. It aims at making people understand (which is laudable) but at the same time suggests that it is spontaneous (which is cheating); it presents itself at once as intentional and irrepressible, artificial and natural, manufactured and discovered. This can lead us to an ethic of signs. Signs ought to present themselves only in two extreme forms: either openly intellectual and so remote that they are reduced to an algebra, as in the Chinese theatre, where a flag on its own signifies a regiment; or deeply rooted, invented, so to speak, on each occasion, revealing an internal, a hidden facet, and indicative of a moment in time, no longer of a concept (as in the art of Stanislavsky, for instance). But the intermediate sign, the fringe of Roman-ness or the sweating of thought, reveals a degraded spectacle, which is equally afraid of simple reality and of total artifice. For although it is a good thing if a spectacle is created to make the world more explicit, it is both reprehensible and deceitful to confuse the sign with what is signified. And it is a duplicity which is peculiar to bourgeois art: between the intellectual and the visceral sign is hypocritically inserted a hybrid, at once elliptical and pretentious, which is pompously christened '*nature*'.

The Writer on Holiday

Gide was reading Bossuet while going down the Congo. This posture sums up rather well the ideal of our writers 'on holiday', as photographed by *Le Figaro*: to add to mere leisure the prestige of a vocation which nothing can stop or degrade. Here is therefore a good piece of journalism, highly efficient sociologically, and which gives us, without cheating, information on the idea which our bourgeoisie entertains about its writers.

What seems above all else to surprise and delight it, then, is its own broad-mindedness in acknowledging that writers too are the sort of people who commonly take holidays. 'Holidays' are a recent social phenomenon, whose mythological development, incidentally, would be interesting to trace. At first a part of the school world, they have become, since the advent of holidays with pay, a part of the proletarian world, or at least the world of working people. To assert that this phenomenon can henceforth concern writers, that the specialists of the human soul are also subjected to the common status of contemporary labour, is a way of convincing our bourgeois readers that they are indeed in step with the times: they pride themselves on acknowledging certain prosaic necessities, they limber up to 'modern' realities through the lessons of Siegfried and Fourastié.

Needless to say, this proletarianization of the writer is granted only with parsimony, the more completely to be destroyed afterwards. No sooner endowed with a social attribute (and holidays are one such attribute, a very agreeable one), the man of letters returns straight away to the empyrean which he shares with the professionals of inspiration. And the 'naturalness' in which our novelists are eternalized is in fact instituted in order to convey a sublime contradiction: between a prosaic condition, produced alas by regrettably materialistic times, and the glamorous status which bourgeois society liberally grants its spiritual representatives (so long as they remain harmless).

What proves the wonderful singularity of the writer, is that during the holiday in question, which he takes alongside factory workers and shop assistants, he unlike them does not stop, if not actually working, at least producing. So that he is a false worker, and a false holiday-maker as well. One is writing his memoirs, another is correcting proofs, yet another is preparing his next book. And he who does nothing confesses it as truly paradoxical behaviour, an avant-garde exploit, which only someone of exceptional independence can afford to flaunt. One then realizes, thanks to this kind of boast, that it is quite 'natural' that the writer should write all the time and in all situations. First, this treats literary production as a sort of involuntary secretion, which is taboo, since it escapes human determinations: to speak more decorously, the writer is the prey of an inner god who speaks at all times, without bothering, tyrant that he is, with the holidays of his medium. Writers are on holiday, but their Muse is awake, and gives birth non-stop.

The second advantage of this logorrhea is that, thanks to its peremptory character, it is quite naturally regarded as the very essence of the writer. True, the latter concedes that he is en-dowed with a human existence, with an old country house, with relatives, with shorts, with a small daughter, etc.; but unlike the other workers, who change their essence, and on the beach are no longer anything but holiday-makers, the writer keeps his writer's nature everywhere. By having holidays, he displays the sign of his being human; but the god remains, one is a writer as Louis XIV was king, even on the commode. Thus the function of the man of letters is to human labour rather as ambrosia is to bread: a miraculous, eternal substance, which condescends to take a social form so that its prestigious difference is better grasped. All this prepares one for the same idea of the writer as a superman, as a kind of intrinsically different being which society puts in the window so as to use to the best advantage the artificial singularity which it has granted him.

The good-natured image of 'the writer on holiday' is therefore no more than one of these cunning mystifications which the Establishment practises the better to enslave its writers. The singularity of a 'vocation' is never better displayed than when it is contradicted — but not denied, far from it — by a prosaic incarnation: this is an old trick of all hagiographies. So that this myth of 'literary holidays' is seen to spread very far, much farther than summer: the techniques of contemporary journalism are devoted more and more to presenting the writer as a prosaic figure. But one would be very wrong to take this as an attempt to demystify. Quite the contrary. True, it may seem touching, and even flattering, that I, a mere reader, should participate, thanks to such confidences, in the daily life of a race selected by genius. I would no doubt feel that a world was blissfully fraternal, in which newspapers told me that a certain great writer wears blue pyjamas, and a certain young novelist has a liking for 'pretty girls, *reblochon* cheese and lavender-honey'. This does not alter the fact that the balance of the operation is that the writer becomes still more charismatic, leaves this earth a little more for a celestial habitat where his pyjamas and his cheeses in no way prevent him from resuming the use of his noble demiurgic speech.

To endow the writer publicly with a good fleshly body, to reveal that he likes dry white wine and underdone steak, is to make even more miraculous for me, and of a more divine essence, the products of his art. Far from the details of his daily life bringing nearer to me the nature of his inspiration and making it clearer, it is the whole mythical singularity of his condition which the writer emphasizes by such confidences. For I cannot but ascribe to some superhumanity the existence of beings vast enough to wear blue pyjamas at the very moment when they manifest themselves as universal conscience, or else make a profession of liking *reblochon* with that same voice with which they announce their forthcoming Phenomenology of the Ego. The spectacular alliance of so much nobility and so much futility means that one still believes in the contradiction: since it is totally miraculous, each of its terms is miraculous too; it would obviously lose all interest in a world where the writer's work was so desacralized that it appeared as natural as his vestimentary or gustatory functions.

The 'Blue Blood' Cruise

Ever since the Coronation, the French had been pining for fresh news about royal activities, of which they are extremely fond; the setting out to sea of a hundred or so royals on a Greek yacht, the *Agamemnon*, entertained them greatly. The Coronation of Elizabeth was a theme which appealed to the emotions and sentimentalities; the 'Blue Blood' Cruise is a humorous episode: kings played at being men, as in a comedy by de Flers and Caillavet; there followed a thousand situations, droll because of contradictions of the Marie-Antoinette-playing-the-milkmaid type. Such a feeling of amusement carries a heavy pathological burden: if one is amused by a contradiction, it is because one supposes its terms to be very far apart. In other words, kings have a superhuman essence, and when they temporarily borrow certain forms of democratic life, it can only be through an incarnation which goes against nature, made possible through condescension alone. To flaunt the fact that kings are capable of prosaic actions is to recognize that this status is no more natural to them than angelism to common mortals, it is to acknowledge that the king is still king by divine right.

Thus the neutral gestures of daily life have taken, on the *Agamemnon*, an exorbitantly bold character, like those creative fantasies in which Nature violates its own kingdoms: kings shave themselves! This touch was reported by our national press as an act of incredible singularity, as if in doing so kings consented to risk the whole of their royal status, making thereby, incidentally, a profession of faith in its indestructible nature. King Paul was wearing an open-neck shirt and short sleeves, Queen Frederika a *print* dress, that is to say one no longer unique but whose pattern can also be seen on the bodies of mere mortals. Formerly, kings dressed up as shepherds; nowadays, to wear for a fortnight clothes from a cheap chain-store is for them the sign of dressing up. Yet another sign of democracy: to get up at six in the morning. All

THE 'BLUE BLOOD' CRUISE

this gives us, antiphrastically, information on a certain ideal of daily life: to wear cuffs, to be shaved by a flunkey, to get up late. By renouncing these privileges, kings make them recede into the heaven of dream: their (very temporary) sacrifice determines and eternalizes the signs of daily bliss.

What is more curious is that this mythical character of our kings is nowadays secularized, though not in the least exorcized, by resorting to scientism of a sort. Kings are defined by the purity of their race (Blue Blood) like puppies, and the ship, the privileged locus of any 'closure', is a kind of modern Ark where the main variations of the monarchic species are preserved. To such an extent that the chances of certain pairings are openly computed. Enclosed in their floating stud-farm, the thorough-breds are sheltered from all mongrel marriages, all is prepared for them (annually, perhaps?) to be able to reproduce among themselves. As small in number as pug-dogs on this earth, the ship immobilizes and gathers them, and constitutes a temporary 'reservation' where an ethnographic curiosity as well protected as a Sioux territory will be kept and, with luck, increased.

The two century-old themes are merged, that of the God-King and that of the King-Object. But this mythological heaven is not as harmless as all that to the Earth. The most ethereal mystifications, the 'amusing details' of the 'Blue Blood' Cruise, all this anecdotal blah with which the national press made its readers drunk is not proffered without damage: confident in their restored divinity, the princes democratically engage in politics. The Comte de Paris leaves the *Agamemnon* and comes to Paris to 'keep close watch' on the fortunes of the European Defence Community, and the young Juan of Spain is sent to the rescue of Spanish Fascism.

33

Blind and Dumb Criticism

Critics (of books or drama) often use two rather singular arguments. The first consists in suddenly deciding that the true subject of criticism is ineffable, and criticism, as a consequence, unnecessary. The other, which also reappears periodically, consists in confessing that one is too stupid, too unenlightened to understand a book reputedly philosophical. A play by Henri Lefebvre on Kierkegaard has thus provoked in our best critics (and I am not speaking about those who openly profess stupidity) a pretended fear of imbecility (the aim of which was obviously to discredit Lefebvre by relegating him to the ridicule of pure intellectualism).

Why do critics thus periodically proclaim their helplessness or their lack of understanding? It is certainly not out of modesty: no one is more at ease than one critic confessing that he understands nothing about existentialism; no one more ironic and therefore more self-assured than another admitting shame-facedly that he does not have the luck to have been initiated into the philosophy of the Extraordinary; and no one more soldier-like than a third pleading for poetic ineffability.

All this means in fact that one believes oneself to have such sureness of intelligence that acknowledging an inability to understand calls in question the clarity of the author and not that of one's own mind. One mimics silliness in order to make the public protest in one's favour, and thus carry it along advantageously from complicity in helplessness to complicity in intelligence. It is an operation well known to salons like Madame Verdurin's:* 'I whose profession it is to be intelligent, understand nothing about it; now you wouldn't understand anything about it either; therefore, it can only be that you are as intelligent as I am.'

The reality behind this seasonally professed lack of culture is the old obscurantist myth according to which ideas are

* In Proust's *A la Recherche du Temps perdu*.

noxious if they are not controlled by 'common sense' and 'feeling': Knowledge is Evil, they both grew on the same tree. Culture is allowed on condition that it periodically proclaims the vanity of its ends and the limits of its power (see also on this subject the ideas of Mr Graham Greene on psychologists and psychiatrists); ideally, culture should be nothing but a sweet rhetorical effusion, an art of using words to bear witness to a transient moistening of the soul. Yet this old romantic couple, the heart and the head, has no reality except in an imagery of vaguely Gnostic origin, in these opiate-like philosophies which have always, in the end, constituted the mainstay of strong regimes, and in which one gets rid of intellectuals by telling them to run along and get on with the emotions and the ineffable. In fact, any reservation about culture means a terrorist position. To be a critic by profession and to proclaim that one understands nothing about existentialism or Marxism (for as it happens, it is these two philosophies particularly that one confesses to be unable to understand) is to elevate one's blindness or dumbness to a universal rule of perception, and to reject from the world Marxism and existentialism: 'I don't understand, therefore you are idiots.'

But if one fears or despises so much the philosophical foundations of a book, and if one demands so insistently the right to understand nothing about them and to say nothing on the subject, why become a critic? To understand, to enlighten, that is your profession, isn't it? You can of course judge philosophy according to common sense; the trouble is that while 'common sense' and 'feeling' understand nothing about philosophy, philosophy, on the other hand, understands them perfectly. You don't explain philosophers, but *they* explain you. You don't want to understand the play by Lefebvre the Marxist, but you can be sure that Lefebvre the Marxist understands your incomprehension perfectly well, and above all (for I believe you to be more wily than lacking in culture) the delightfully 'harmless' confession you make of it.

Soap-powders and Detergents

The first World Detergent Congress (Paris, September 1954) had the effect of authorizing the world to yield to *Omo* euphoria: not only do detergents have no harmful effect on the skin, but they can even perhaps save miners from silicosis. These products have been in the last few years the object of such massive advertising that they now belong to a region of French daily life which the various types of psycho-analysis would do well to pay some attention to if they wish to keep up to date. One could then usefully contrast the psycho-analysis of purifying fluids (chlorinated, for example) with that of soap-powders (*Lux*, *Persil*) or that of detergents (*Omo*). The relations between the evil and the cure, between dirt and a given product, are very different in each case.

Chlorinated fluids, for instance, have always been experienced as a sort of liquid fire, the action of which must be carefully estimated, otherwise the object itself would be affected, 'burnt'. The implicit legend of this type of product rests on the idea of a violent, abrasive modification of matter: the connotations are of a chemical or mutilating type: the product 'kills' the dirt. Powders, on the contrary, are separating agents: their ideal role is to liberate the object from its circumstantial imperfection: dirt is 'forced out' and no longer killed; in the *Omo* imagery, dirt is a diminutive enemy, stunted and black, which takes to its heels from the fine immaculate linen at the sole threat of the judgment of *Omo*. Products based on chlorine and ammonia are without doubt the representatives of a kind of absolute fire, a saviour but a blind one. Powders, on the contrary, are selective, they push, they drive dirt through the texture of the object, their function is keeping public order not making war. This distinction has ethnographic correlatives: the chemical fluid is an extension of the washerwoman's movements when she beats the clothes, while powders rather replace those of the housewife pressing and rolling the washing against a sloping board.

But even in the category of powders, one must in addition oppose against advertisements based on psychology those based on psycho-analysis (I use this word without reference to any specific school). '*Persil* Whiteness' for instance, bases its prestige on the evidence of a result; it calls into play vanity, a social concern with appearances, by offering for comparison two objects, one of which is *whiter than* the other. Advertisements for *Omo* also indicate the effect of the product (and in superlative fashion, incidentally), but they chiefly reveal its mode of action; in doing so, they involve the consumer in a kind of direct experience of the substance, make him the accomplice of a liberation rather than the mere beneficiary of a result; matter here is endowed with value-bearing states.

Omo uses two of these, which are rather novel in the category of detergents: the deep and the foamy. To say that *Omo* cleans in depth (see the Cinéma-Publicité advertisement) is to assume that linen is deep, which no one had previously thought, and this unquestionably results in exalting it, by establishing it as an object favourable to those obscure tendencies to enfold and caress which are found in every human body. As for foam, it is well known that it signifies luxury. To begin with, it appears to lack any usefulness; then, its abundant, easy, almost infinite proliferation allows one to suppose there is in the substance from which it issues a vigorous germ, a healthy and powerful essence, a great wealth of active elements in a small original volume. Finally, it gratifies in the consumer a tendency to imagine matter as something airy, with which contact is effected in a mode both light and vertical, which is sought after like that of happiness either in the gustatory category (foie gras, entremets, wines), in that of clothing (muslin, tulle), or that of soaps (film-star in her bath). Foam can even be the sign of a certain spirituality, inasmuch as the spirit has the reputation of being able to make something out of nothing, a large surface of effects out of a small volume of causes (creams have a very different 'psycho-analytical' meaning, of a soothing kind: they suppress wrinkles, pain, smarting, etc.). What matters is the art of having disguised the abrasive function of the detergent under the delicious image of a substance at once deep and airy which can govern the molecular order of the material without damaging it. A euphoria, incidentally, which must not make us forget that there is one plane on which *Persil* and *Omo* are one and the same: the plane of the Anglo-Dutch trust *Unilever*.

The Poor and the Proletariat

Charlie Chaplin's latest gag has been to transfer half of his Soviet prize into the funds of the Abbé Pierre. At bottom, this amounts to establishing an identity between the nature of the poor man and that of the proletarian. Chaplin has always seen the proletarian under the guise of the poor man: hence the broadly human force of his representations but also their political ambiguity. This is quite evident in this admirable film, *Modern Times*, in which he repeatedly approaches the proletarian theme, but never endorses it politically. What he presents us with is the proletarian still blind and mystified, defined by the immediate character of his needs, and his total alienation at the hands of his masters (the employers and the police).

For Chaplin, the proletarian is still the man who is hungry; the representations of hunger are always epic with him: excessive size of the sandwiches, rivers of milk, fruit which one tosses aside hardly touched. Ironically, the food-dispensing machine (which is part of the employers' world) delivers only fragmented and obviously flavourless nutriment. Ensnared in his starvation, Chaplin-Man is always just below political awareness. A strike is a catastrophe for him because it threatens a man truly blinded by his hunger; this man achieves an awareness of the working-class condition only when the poor man and the proletarian coincide under the gaze (and the blows) of the police. Historically, Man according to Chaplin roughly corresponds to the worker of the French Restoration, rebelling against the machines, at a loss before strikes, fascinated by the problem of bread-winning (in the literal sense of the word), but as yet unable to reach a knowledge of political causes and an insistence on a collective strategy.

But it is precisely because Chaplin portrays a kind of primitive proletarian, still outside Revolution, that the representative force of the latter is immense. No socialist work has yet succeeded in expressing the humiliated condition of the worker with so much violence and generosity. Brecht alone, perhaps, has glimpsed the necessity, for socialist art, of always taking Man on the eve of Revolution, that is to say, alone, still blind, on the point of having his eyes opened to the revolutionary light by the 'natural' excess of his wretchedness. Other works, in showing the worker already engaged in a conscious fight, subsumed under the Cause and the Party, give an account of a political reality which is necessary, but lacks aesthetic force.

Now Chaplin, in conformity with Brecht's idea, shows the public its blindness by presenting at the same time a man who is blind and what is in front of him. To see someone who does not see is the best way to be intensely aware of *what* he does not see: thus, at a Punch and Judy show, it is the children who announce to Punch what he pretends not to see. For instance, Charlie Chaplin is in a cell, pampered by the warders, and lives there according to the ideal of the American petit-bourgeois: with legs crossed, he reads the paper under a portrait of Lincoln; but his delightfully self-satisfied posture discredits this ideal completely, so that it is no longer possible for anyone to take refuge in it without noticing the new alienation which it contains. The slightest ensnarements are thus made harmless, and the man who is poor is repeatedly cut off from temptation. All told, it is perhaps because of this that Chaplin-Man triumphs over everything: because he escapes from everything, eschews any kind of sleeping partner, and never invests in man anything but man himself. His anarchy, politically open to discussion, perhaps represents the most efficient form of revolution in the realm of art.

Operation Margarine

To instil into the Established Order the complacent portrayal of its drawbacks has nowadays become a paradoxical but incontrovertible means of exalting it. Here is the pattern of this new-style demonstration: take the established value which you want to restore or develop, and first lavishly display its pettiness, the injustices which it produces, the vexations to which it gives rise, and plunge it into its natural imperfection; then, at the last moment, save it *in spite of*, or rather *by* the heavy curse of its blemishes. Some examples? There is no lack of them.

Take the Army; show without disguise its chiefs as martinets, its discipline as narrow-minded and unfair, and into this stupid tyranny immerse an average human being, fallible but likeable, the archetype of the spectator. And then, at the last moment, turn over the magical hat, and pull out of it the image of an army, flags flying, triumphant, bewitching, to which, like Sganarelle's wife,[1] one cannot but be faithful although beaten (*From here to eternity*).

Take the Army again: lay down as a basic principle the scientific fanaticism of its engineers, and their blindness; show all that is destroyed by such a pitiless rigour: human beings, couples. And then bring out the flag, save the army in the name of progress, hitch the greatness of the former to the triumph of the latter (*Les Cyclones*, by Jules Roy).

Finally, the Church: speak with burning zeal about its self-righteousness, the narrow-mindedness of its bigots, indicate that all this can be murderous, hide none of the weaknesses of the faith. And then, *in extremis*, hint that the letter of the law, however unattractive, is a way to salvation for its very victims, and so justify moral austerity by the saintliness of those whom it crushes (*The Living Room*, by Graham Greene).

It is a kind of homeopathy: one cures doubts about the

[1] In Molière's *Médecin malgré lui*.

Church or the Army by the very ills of the Church and the Army. One inoculates the public with a contingent evil to prevent or cure an essential one. To rebel against the inhumanity of the Established Order and its values, according to this way of thinking, is an illness which is common, natural, forgivable; one must not collide with it head-on, but rather exorcize it like a possession: the patient is made to give a representation of his illness, he is made familiar with the very appearance of his revolt, and this revolt disappears all the more surely since, once at a distance and the object of a gaze, the Established Order is no longer anything but a Manichaean compound and therefore inevitable, one which wins on both counts, and is therefore beneficial. The immanent evil of enslavement is redeemed by the transcendent good of religion, fatherland, the Church, etc. A little 'confessed' evil saves one from acknowledging a lot of hidden evil.

One can trace in advertising a narrative pattern which clearly shows the working of this new vaccine. It is found in the publicity for *Astra* margarine. The episode always begins with a cry of indignation against margarine: 'A mousse? Made with margarine? Unthinkable!' 'Margarine? Your uncle will be furious!' And then one's eyes are opened, one's conscience becomes more pliable, and margarine is a delicious food, tasty, digestible, economical, useful in all circumstances. The moral at the end is well known: 'Here you are, rid of a prejudice which cost you dearly!' It is in the same way that the Established Order relieves you of your progressive prejudices. The Army, an absolute value? It is unthinkable: look at its vexations, its strictness, the always possible blindness of its chiefs. The Church, infallible? Alas, it is very doubtful: look at its bigots, its powerless priests, its murderous conformism. And then common sense makes its reckoning: what is this trifling dross of Order, compared to its advantages? It is well worth the price of an immunization. What does it matter, *after all*, if margarine is just fat, when it goes further than butter, and costs less? What does it matter, *after all*, if Order is a little brutal or a little blind, when it allows us to live cheaply? Here we are, in our turn, rid of a prejudice which cost us dearly, too dearly, which cost us too much in scruples, in revolt, in fights and in solitude.

Dominici, or the Triumph of Literature

The whole Dominici trial* was enacted according to a certain
idea of psychology, which happens to be, as luck would have it,
that of the Literature of the bourgeois Establishment. Since
material evidence was uncertain or contradictory, one had to
resort to evidence of a mental kind; and where could one find it,
except in the very mentality of the accusers? The motives and
sequence of actions were therefore reconstituted off-hand but
without a shadow of a doubt; in the manner of those archaeo-
logists who go and gather old stones all over the excavation site
and with their cement, modern as it is, erect a delicate wayside
altar of Sesostris, or else, who reconstitute a religion which has
been dead for two thousand years by drawing on the ancient
fund of universal wisdom, which is in fact nothing but their own
brand of wisdom, elaborated in the schools of the Third
Republic.

The same applies to the 'psychology' of old Dominici. Is it
really his? No one knows. But one can be sure that it is indeed
that of the Presiding Judge of the Assizes or the Public Prosecutor.
Do these two mentalities, that of the old peasant from the Alps
and that of the judiciary, function in the same way? Nothing is
less likely. And yet it is in the name of a 'universal' psychology
that old Dominici has been condemned: descending from the
charming empyrean of bourgeois novels and essentialist psychology, Literature has just condemned a man to the guillotine.
Listen to the Public Prosecutor: '*Sir Jack Drummond, I told you,
was afraid. But he knows that in the end the best way to defend
oneself is to attack. So he throws himself on this fierce-looking man
and takes the old man by the throat. Not a word is spoken. But to
Gaston Dominici, the simple fact that someone should want to hold*

* Gaston Dominici, the 80-year-old owner of the Grand'Terre farm in Provence,
was convicted in 1952 of murdering Sir Jack Drummond, his wife and daughter,
whom he found camping near his land.

him down by both shoulders is unthinkable. It was physically impossible for him to bear this strength which was suddenly pitted against him.' This is credible like the temple of Sesostris, like the Literature of M. Genevoix. Only, to base archaeology or the novel on a 'Why not?' does not harm anybody. But Justice? Periodically, some trial, and not necessarily fictitious like the one in Camus's *The Outsider*, comes to remind you that the Law is always prepared to lend you a spare brain in order to condemn you without remorse, and that, like Corneille, it depicts you as you should be, and not as you are.

This official visit of Justice to the world of the accused is made possible thanks to an intermediate myth which is always used abundantly by all official institutions, whether they are the Assizes or the periodicals of literary sects: the transparence and universality of language. The Presiding Judge of the Assizes, who reads *Le Figaro*, has obviously no scruples in exchanging words with the old 'uneducated' goatherd. Do they not have in common the same language, and the clearest there is, French? O wonderful self-assurance of classical education, in which shepherds, without embarrassment, converse with judges! But here again, behind the prestigious (and grotesque) morality of Latin translations and essays in French, what is at stake is the head of a man.

And yet the disparity of both languages, their impenetrability to each other, have been stressed by a few journalists, and Giono has given numerous examples of this in his accounts of the trial. Their remarks show that there is no need to imagine mysterious barriers, Kafka-like misunderstandings. No: syntax, vocabulary, most of the elementary, analytical materials of language grope blindly without ever touching, but no one has any qualms about it ('*Êtes-vous allé au pont?*— *Allée? il n'y a pas d'allée, je le sais, j'y suis été*').* Naturally, everyone pretends to believe that it is the official language which is common sense, that of Dominici being only one of its ethnological varieties, picturesque in its poverty. And yet, this language of the president is just as peculiar, laden

---

* 'Did you go to the bridge?—A path? There is no path, I know, I've been there!' *Allé* = 'gone', *allée* = a path, but Dominici uses *été*, 'been'.

as it is with unreal clichés; it is a language for school essays, not for a concrete psychology (but perhaps it is unavoidable for most men, alas, to have the psychology of the language which they have been taught). These are in actual fact two particular uses of language which confront each other. But one of them has honours, law and force on its side.

And this 'universal' language comes just at the right time to lend a new strength to the psychology of the masters: it allows it always to take other men as objects, to describe and condemn at one stroke. It is an adjectival psychology, it knows only how to endow its victims with epithets, it is ignorant of everything about the actions themselves, save the guilty category into which they are forcibly made to fit. These categories are none other than those of classical comedy or treatises of graphology: boastful, irascible, selfish, cunning, lecherous, harsh, man exists in their eyes only through the 'character traits' which label him for society as the object of a more or less easy absorption, the subject of a more or less respectful submission. Utilitarian, taking no account of any state of consciousness, this psychology has nevertheless the pretension of giving as a basis for actions a pre-existing inner person, it postulates 'the soul': it judges man as a 'conscience' without being embarrassed by having previously described him as an object.

Now that particular psychology, in the name of which you can very well today have your head cut off, comes straight from our traditional literature, that which one calls in bourgeois style literature of the Human Document. It is in the name of the human document that the old Dominici has been condemned. Justice and literature have made an alliance, they have exchanged their old techniques, thus revealing their basic identity, and com-promising each other barefacedly. Behind the judges, in curule chairs, the writers (Giono, Salacrou). And on the prosecution side, do we see a lawyer? No, an 'extraordinary story-teller', gifted with 'undeniable wit' and a 'dazzling verve' (to quote the shocking testimonial granted to the public prosecutor by *Le Monde*). Even the police is here seen practising fine writing (Police Superintendent: '*Never have I met such a dissembling liar, such a wary gambler, such a witty narrator, such a wily trickster, such a lusty septuagenarian, such a self-assured despot, such a devious schemer, such a cunning hypocrite ... Gaston Dominici is an astonishing quick-change artist playing with human souls, and animal thoughts ... This false patriarch of the Grand'Terre has not just a few facets, he has a hundred!'*). Antithesis, metaphors, flights of oratory, it is the whole of classical rhetoric which accuses the old shepherd here. Justice took the mask of Realist literature, of the country tale, while literature itself came to the court-room to gather new 'human' documents, and naively to seek from the face of the accused and the suspects the reflection of a psychology which, however, it had been the first to impose on them by the arm of the law.

Only, confronting the literature of repletion (which is always passed off as the literature of the 'real' and the 'human'), there is a literature of poignancy; the Dominici trial has also been this type of literature. There have not been here only writers hungering for reality and brilliant narrators whose 'dazzling' verve carries off a man's head; whatever the degree of guilt of the accused, there was also the spectacle of a terror which threatens us all, that of being judged by a power which wants to hear only the language it lends us. We are all potential Dominicis, not as murderers but as accused, deprived of language, or worse, rigged out in that of our accusers, humiliated and condemned by it. To rob a man of his language in the very name of language: this is the first step in all legal murders.

The Iconography of the Abbé Pierre

The myth of the Abbé Pierre has at its disposal a precious asset: the physiognomy of the Abbé. It is a fine physiognomy, which clearly displays all the signs of apostleship: a benign expression, a Franciscan haircut, a missionary's beard, all this made complete by the sheepskin coat of the worker-priest and the staff of the pilgrim. Thus are united the marks of legend and those of modernity.

The haircut, for example, half shorn, devoid of affectation and above all of definite shape, is without doubt trying to achieve a style completely outside the bounds of art and even of technique, a sort of zero degree of haircut. One has to have one's hair cut, of course; but at least, let this necessary operation imply no particular mode of existence: let it exist, but let it not be anything in particular. The Abbé Pierre's haircut, obviously devised so as to reach a neutral equilibrium between short hair (an indispensable convention if one does not want to be noticed) and unkempt hair (a state suitable to express contempt for other conventions), thus becomes the capillary archetype of saintliness: the saint is first and foremost a being without formal context; the idea of fashion is antipathetic to the idea of sainthood.

But at this point things get more complicated—unknown to the Abbé, one hopes—because here as everywhere else, neutrality ends up by functioning as the *sign* of neutrality, and if you really wished to go unnoticed, you would be back where you started. The 'zero' haircut, then, is quite simply the label of Franciscanism; first conceived negatively so as not to contradict the appearance of sainthood, it quickly becomes a superlative mode of signification, it *dresses up* the Abbé as Saint Francis. Hence the tremendous iconographic popularity of this haircut in illustrated magazines and in films (where Reybaz the actor will have but to adopt it to be completely identified with the Abbé).

The beard goes through the same mythological routine. True, it can simply be the attribute of a free man, detached from the daily conventions of our world and who shrinks from wasting time in shaving: fascination with charity may well be expected to result in this type of contempt; but we are forced to notice that ecclesiastical beards also have a little mythology of their own. For among priests, it is not due to chance whether one is bearded or not; beards are chiefly the attribute of missionaries or Capuchins, they cannot but *signify* apostleship and poverty. They withdraw their bearers a little from the secular clergy. Shaven priests are supposed to be more temporal, bearded ones more evangelical: the wicked Frolo was beardless,* the good Père de Foucauld bearded. Behind a beard, one belongs a little less to one's bishop, to the hierarchy, to the Church as a political force; one looks freer, a bit of an independent, more primitive in short, benefiting from the prestige of the first hermits, enjoying the blunt candour of the founders of monastic life, the depositories of the spirit against the letter: wearing a beard means exploring in the same spirit the slums, the land of the early Britons or Nyasaland.

Naturally, the problem is not to know how this forest of *signs* has been able to grow on the Abbé Pierre (although it is indeed surprising that the attributes of goodness should be like transferable coins allowing an easy exchange between reality (the Abbé Pierre of *Match*) and fiction (the Abbé Pierre of the film) and that, in short, apostleship should appear from the start ready-made and fully equipped for the big journey of reconstitutions and legends). I am only wondering about the enormous consumption of such signs by the public. I see it reassured by the spectacular identity of a morphology and a vocation, in no doubt about the latter because it knows the former, no longer having access to the real experience of apostleship except through the bric-à-brac associated with it, and getting used to acquiring a clear conscience by merely looking at the shop-window of saintliness; and I get worried about a society which consumes with such avidity the display of charity that it forgets to ask itself questions about its consequences, its uses and its limits. And I

* In Victor Hugo's *Notre-Dame de Paris*.

then start to wonder whether the fine and touching iconography of the Abbé Pierre is not the alibi which a sizeable part of the nation uses in order, once more, to substitute with impunity the signs of charity for the reality of justice.

Novels and Children

If we are to believe the weekly *Elle*, which some time ago mustered seventy women novelists on one photograph, the woman of letters is a remarkable zoological species: she brings forth, pell-mell, novels and children. We are introduced, for example, to *Jacqueline Lenoir (two daughters, one novel); Marina Grey (one son, one novel); Nicole Dutreil (two sons, four novels)*, etc.

What does it mean? This: to write is a glorious but bold activity; the writer is an 'artist', one recognizes that he is entitled to a little bohemianism. As he is in general entrusted — at least in the France of *Elle* — with giving society reasons for its clear conscience, he must, after all, be paid for his services: one tacitly grants him the right to some individuality. But make no mistake: let no women believe that they can take advantage of this pact without having first submitted to the eternal statute of womanhood. Women are on the earth to give children to men; let them write as much as they like, let them decorate their condition, but above all, let them not depart from it: let their Biblical fate not be disturbed by the promotion which is conceded to them, and let them pay immediately, by the tribute of their motherhood, for this bohemianism which has a natural link with a writer's life.

Women, be therefore courageous, free; play at being men, write like them; but never get far from them; live under their gaze, compensate for your books by your children; enjoy a free rein for a while, but quickly come back to your condition. One novel, one child, a little feminism, a little connubiality. Let us tie the adventure of art to the strong pillars of the home: both will profit a great deal from this combination: where myths are concerned, mutual help is always fruitful.

For instance, the Muse will give its sublimity to the humble tasks of the home; and in exchange, to thank her for this favour, the myth of child-bearing will lend to the Muse, who sometimes has the reputation of being a little wanton, the guarantee of its respectability, the touching decor of the nursery. So that all is well in the best of all worlds—that of *Elle*. Let women acquire self-confidence: they can very well have access, like men, to the superior status of creation. But let men be quickly reassured: women will not be taken from them for all that, they will remain no less available for motherhood by nature. *Elle* nimbly plays a Molièresque scene, says yes on one side and no on the other, and busies herself in displeasing no one; like Don Juan between his two peasant girls, *Elle* says to women: you are worth just as much as men; and to men: your women will never be anything but women.

Man at first seems absent from this double parturition; children and novels alike seem to come by themselves, and to belong to the mother alone. At a pinch, and by dint of seeing seventy times books and kids bracketed together, one would think that they are equally the fruits of imagination and dream, the miraculous products of an ideal parthenogenesis able to give at once to woman, apparently, the Balzacian joys of creation and the tender joys of motherhood. Where then is man in this family picture? Nowhere and everywhere, like the sky, the horizon, an authority which at once determines and limits a condition. Such is the world of *Elle*: women there are always a homogeneous species, an established body jealous of its privileges, still more enamoured of the burdens that go with them. Man is never inside, femininity is pure, free, powerful; but man is everywhere around, he presses on all sides, he makes everything exist; he is in all eternity the creative absence, that of the Racinian deity: the feminine world of *Elle*, a world without men, but entirely constituted by the gaze of man, is very exactly that of the gynaeceum.

In every feature of *Elle* we find this twofold action: lock the gynaeceum, then and only then release woman inside. Love, work, write, be business-women or women of letters, but always remember that man exists, and that you are not made like him; your order is free on condition that it depends on his; your freedom is a luxury, it is possible only if you first acknowledge the obligations of your nature. Write, if you want to, we women shall all be very proud of it; but don't forget on the other hand to produce children, for that is your destiny. A Jesuitic morality: adapt the moral rule of your condition, but never compromise about the dogma on which it rests.

Toys

French toys: one could not find a better illustration of the fact that the adult Frenchman sees the child as another self. All the toys one commonly sees are essentially a microcosm of the adult world; they are all reduced copies of human objects, as if in the eyes of the public the child was, all told, nothing but a smaller man, a homunculus to whom must be supplied objects of his own size.

Invented forms are very rare: a few sets of blocks, which appeal to the spirit of do-it-yourself, are the only ones which offer dynamic forms. As for the others, French toys *always mean something*, and this something is always entirely socialized, constituted by the myths or the techniques of modern adult life: the Army, Broadcasting, the Post Office, Medicine (miniature instrument-cases, operating theatres for dolls), School, Hair-Styling (driers for permanent-waving), the Air Force (Parachutists), Transport (trains, Citroëns, Vedettes, Vespas, petrol-stations), Science (Martian toys).

The fact that French toys *literally* prefigure the world of adult functions obviously cannot but prepare the child to accept them all, by constituting for him, even before he can think about it, the alibi of a Nature which has at all times created soldiers, postmen and Vespas. Toys here reveal the list of all the things the adult does not find unusual: war, bureaucracy, ugliness, Martians, etc. It is not so much, in fact, the imitation which is the sign of an abdication, as its literalness: French toys are like a Jivaro head, in which one recognizes, shrunken to the size of an apple, the wrinkles and hair of an adult. There exist, for instance, dolls which urinate; they have an oesophagus, one gives them a bottle, they wet their nappies; soon, no doubt, milk will turn to water in their stomachs. This is meant to prepare the little girl for the causality of house-keeping, to 'condition' her to her future role as mother. However, faced with this world of faithful and complicated objects, the child can only identify himself as owner, as user, never as creator; he does not invent the world, he uses it: there are, prepared for him, actions without adventure, without wonder, without joy. He is turned into a little stay-at-home householder who does not even have to invent the mainsprings of adult causality; they are supplied to him ready-made: he has only to help himself, he is never allowed to discover anything from start to finish. The merest set of blocks, provided it is not too refined, implies a very different learning of the world: then, the child does not in any way create meaningful objects, it matters little to him whether they have an adult name; the actions he performs are not those of a user but those of a demiurge. He creates forms which walk, which roll, he creates life, not property: objects now act by themselves, they are no longer an inert and complicated material in the palm of his hand. But such toys are rather rare: French toys are usually based on imitation, they are meant to produce children who are users, not creators.

The bourgeois status of toys can be recognized not only in their forms, which are all functional, but also in their substances. Current toys are made of a graceless material, the product of chemistry, not of nature. Many are now moulded from complicated mixtures; the plastic material of which they are made has an appearance at once gross and hygienic, it destroys all the pleasure, the sweetness, the humanity of touch. A sign which fills one with consternation is the gradual disappearance of wood, in spite of its being an ideal material because of its firmness and its softness, and the natural warmth of its touch. Wood removes, from all the forms which it supports, the wounding quality of angles which are too sharp, the chemical coldness of metal. When the child handles it and knocks it, it neither vibrates nor grates, it has a sound at once muffled and sharp. It is a familiar and poetic substance, which does not sever the child from close contact with the tree, the table, the floor. Wood does not wound or break down; it does not shatter, it wears out, it can last a long time, live with the child, alter little by little the relations between the object and the hand. If it dies, it is in dwindling, not in swelling out like those mechanical toys which disappear behind the hernia of a broken spring. Wood makes essential objects, objects for all time. Yet there hardly remain any of these wooden toys from the Vosges, these fretwork farms with their animals, which were only possible, it is true, in the days of the craftsman. Henceforth, toys are chemical in substance and colour; their very material introduces one to a coenaesthesis of use, not pleasure. These toys die in fact very quickly, and once dead, they have no posthumous life for the child.

The Face of Garbo

Garbo still belongs to that moment in cinema when capturing the human face still plunged audiences into the deepest ecstasy, when one literally lost oneself in a human image as one would in a philtre, when the face represented a kind of absolute state of the flesh, which could be neither reached nor renounced. A few years earlier the face of Valentino was causing suicides; that of Garbo still partakes of the same rule of Courtly Love, where the flesh gives rise to mystical feelings of perdition.

It is indeed an admirable face-object. In *Queen Christina*, a film which has again been shown in Paris in the last few years, the make-up has the snowy thickness of a mask: it is not a painted face, but one set in plaster, protected by the surface of the colour, not by its lineaments. Amid all this snow at once fragile and compact, the eyes alone, black like strange soft flesh, but not in the least expressive, are two faintly tremulous wounds. In spite of its extreme beauty, this face, not drawn but sculpted in something smooth and friable, that is, at once perfect and ephemeral, comes to resemble the flour-white complexion of Charlie Chaplin, the dark vegetation of his eyes, his totem-like countenance.

Now the temptation of the absolute mask (the mask of antiquity, for instance) perhaps implies less the theme of the secret (as is the case with Italian half mask) than that of an archetype of the human face. Garbo offered to one's gaze a sort of Platonic Idea of the human creature, which explains why her face is almost sexually undefined, without however leaving one in doubt. It is true that this film (in which Queen Christina is by turns a woman and a young cavalier) lends itself to this lack of differentiation; but Garbo does not perform in it any feat of transvestism; she is always herself, and carries without pretence, under her crown or her wide-brimmed hats, the same snowy solitary face. The name given to her, *the Divine*, probably aimed to convey less a superlative state of beauty than the essence of her corporeal person, descended from a heaven where all things are formed and perfected in the clearest light. She herself knew this: how many actresses have consented to let the crowd see the ominous maturing of their beauty. Not she, however; the essence was not to be degraded, her face was not to have any reality except that of its perfection, which was intellectual even more than formal. The Essence became gradually obscured, progressively veiled with dark glasses, broad hats and exiles: but it never deteriorated.

And yet, in this deified face, something sharper than a mask is looming: a kind of voluntary and therefore human relation between the curve of the nostrils and the arch of the eyebrows; a rare, individual function relating two regions of the face. A mask is but a sum of lines; a face, on the contrary, is above all their thematic harmony. Garbo's face represents this fragile moment when the cinema is about to draw an existential from an essential beauty, when the archetype leans towards the fascination of mortal faces, when the clarity of the flesh as essence yields its place to a lyricism of Woman.

Viewed as a transition the face of Garbo reconciles two iconographic ages, it assures the passage from awe to charm. As is well known, we are today at the other pole of this evolution: the face of Audrey Hepburn, for instance, is individualized, not only because of its peculiar thematics (woman as child, woman as kitten) but also because of her person, of an almost unique specification of the face, which has nothing of the essence left in it, but is constituted by an infinite complexity of morphological functions. As a language, Garbo's singularity was of the order of the concept, that of Audrey Hepburn is of the order of the substance. The face of Garbo is an Idea, that of Hepburn, an Event.

Wine and Milk

Wine is felt by the French nation to be a possession which is its very own, just like its three hundred and sixty types of cheese and its culture. It is a totem-drink, corresponding to the milk of the Dutch cow or the tea ceremonially taken by the British Royal Family. Bachelard has already given the 'substantial psycho-analysis' of this fluid, at the end of his essay on the reveries on the theme of the will, and shown that wine is the sap of the sun and the earth, that its basic state is not the moist but the dry, and that on such grounds the substance which is most contrary to it is water.

Actually, like all resilient totems, wine supports a varied mythology which does not trouble about contradictions. This galvanic substance is always considered, for instance, as the most efficient of thirst-quenchers, or at least this serves as the major alibi for its consumption ('It's thirsty weather'). In its red form, it has blood, the dense and vital fluid, as a very old hypo-stasis. This is because in fact its humoral form matters little; it is above all a converting substance, capable of reversing situations and states, and of extracting from objects their opposites – for instance, making a weak man strong or a silent one talkative. Hence its old alchemical heredity, its philosophical power to transmute and create *ex nihilo*.

Being essentially a function whose terms can change, wine has at its disposal apparently plastic powers: it can serve as an alibi to dream as well as reality, it depends on the users of the myth. For the worker, wine means enabling him to do his task with demiurgic ease ('heart for the work'). For the intellectual, wine has the reverse function: the local white wine or the beaujolais of the writer is meant to cut him off from the all too expected environment of cocktails and expensive drinks (the only ones which snobbishness leads one to offer him). Wine will deliver him from myths, will remove some of his intellectualism, will make him the equal of the proletarian; through wine, the intellectual comes nearer to a natural virility, and believes he can thus escape the curse that a century and a half of romanticism still brings to bear on the purely cerebral (it is well known that one of the myths peculiar to the modern intellectual is the obsession to 'have it where it matters').

But what is characteristic of France is that the converting power of wine is never openly presented as an end. Other countries drink to get drunk, and this is accepted by everyone; in France, drunkenness is a consequence, never an intention. A drink is felt as the spinning out of a pleasure, not as the necessary cause of an effect which is sought: wine is not only a philtre, it is also the leisurely act of drinking. The *gesture* has here a decorative value, and the power of wine is never separated from its modes of existence (unlike whisky, for example, which is drunk for its type of drunkenness — 'the most agreeable, with the least painful after-effects' — which one gulps down repeatedly, and the drinking of which is reduced to a causal act).

All this is well known and has been said a thousand times in folklore, proverbs, conversations and Literature. But this very universality implies a kind of conformism: to believe in wine is a coercive collective act. A Frenchman who kept this myth at arm's length would expose himself to minor but definite problems of integration, the first of which, precisely, would be that of having to explain his attitude. The universality principle fully applies here, inasmuch as society calls anyone who does not believe in wine by *names* such as sick, disabled or depraved: it does not *comprehend* him (in both senses, intellectual and spatial, of the word). Conversely, an award of good integration is given to whoever is a practising wine-drinker: knowing *how* to drink is a national technique which serves to qualify the Frenchman, to demonstrate at once his performance, his control and his sociability. Wine gives thus a foundation for a collective morality, within which everything is redeemed: true, excesses, misfortunes and crimes are possible with wine, but never viciousness, treachery or baseness; the evil it can generate is in the nature of fate and therefore escapes penalization, it evokes the theatre rather than a basic temperament.

Wine is a part of society because it provides a basis not only for a morality but also for an environment; it is an ornament in the slightest ceremonials of French daily life, from the snack (plonk and camembert) to the feast, from the conversation at the local café to the speech at a formal dinner. It exalts all climates, of whatever kind: in cold weather, it is associated with all the myths of becoming warm, and at the height of summer, with all the images of shade, with all things cool and sparkling. There is no situation involving some physical constraint (temperature, hunger, boredom, compulsion, disorientation) which does not give rise to dreams of wine. Combined as a basic substance with other alimentary figures, it can cover all the aspects of space and time for the Frenchman. As soon as one gets to know someone's daily life fairly well, the absence of wine gives a sense of shock, like something exotic: M. Coty, having allowed himself to be photographed, at the beginning of his seven years' presidency, sitting at home before a table on which a bottle of beer seemed to replace, by an extraordinary exception, the familiar litre of red wine, the whole nation was in a flutter; it was as intolerable as having a bachelor king. Wine is here a part of the reason of state.

Bachelard was probably right in seeing water as the opposite of wine: mythically, this is true; sociologically, today at least, less so; economic and historical circumstances have given this part to milk. The latter is now the true anti-wine: and not only because of M. Mendès-France's popularizing efforts (which had a purposely mythological look as when he used to drink milk during his speeches in the Chamber, as Popeye eats spinach), but also because in the basic morphology of substances milk is the opposite of fire by all the denseness of its molecules, by the creamy, and therefore soothing, nature of its spreading. Wine is mutilating, surgical, it transmutes and delivers; milk is cosmetic, it joins, covers, restores. Moreover, its purity, associated with the innocence of the child, is a token of strength, of a strength which is not revulsive, not congestive, but calm, white, lucid, the equal of reality. Some American films, in which the hero, strong and uncompromising, did not shrink from having a glass of milk before drawing his avenging Colt, have paved the way for this new Parsifalian myth. A strange mixture of milk and pomegranate, originating in America, is to this day sometimes drunk in Paris, among gangsters and hoodlums. But milk remains an exotic substance; it is wine which is part of the nation.

The mythology of wine can in fact help us to understand the usual ambiguity of our daily life. For it is true that wine is a good and fine substance, but it is no less true that its production is deeply involved in French capitalism, whether it is that of the private distillers or that of the big settlers in Algeria who impose on the Muslims, on the very land of which they have been dispossessed, a crop of which they have no need, while they lack even bread. There are thus very engaging myths which are however not innocent. And the characteristic of our current alienation is precisely that wine cannot be an unalloyedly blissful substance, except if we wrongfully forget that it is also the product of an expropriation.

Steak and Chips

Steak is a part of the same sanguine mythology as wine. It is the heart of meat, it is meat in its pure state; and whoever partakes of it assimilates a bull-like strength. The prestige of steak evidently derives from its quasi-rawness. In it, blood is visible, natural, dense, at once compact and sectile. One can well imagine the ambrosia of the Ancients as this kind of heavy substance which dwindles under one's teeth in such a way as to make one keenly aware at the same time of its original strength and of its aptitude to flow into the very blood of man. Full-bloodedness is the raison d'être of steak; the degrees to which it is cooked are expressed not in calorific units but in images of blood; rare steak is said to be *saignant* (when it recalls the arterial flow from the cut in the animal's throat), or *bleu* (and it is now the heavy, plethoric, blood of the veins which is suggested by the purplish colour — the superlative of redness). Its cooking, even moderate, cannot openly find expression; for this unnatural state, a euphemism is needed: one says that steak is *à point*, 'medium', and this in truth is understood more as a limit than as a perfection.

To eat steak rare therefore represents both a nature and a morality. It is supposed to benefit all the temperaments, the sanguine because it is identical, the nervous and lymphatic because it is complementary to them. And just as wine becomes for a good number of intellectuals a mediumistic substance which leads them towards the original strength of nature, steak is for them a redeeming food, thanks to which they bring their intellectualism to the level of prose and exorcize, through blood and soft pulp, the sterile dryness of which they are constantly accused. The craze for steak tartare, for instance, is a magic spell against the romantic association between sensitiveness and sickliness; there are to be found, in this preparation, all the germinating states of matter: the blood mash and the glair of eggs, a whole harmony of soft and life-giving substances, a sort of meaningful compendium of the images of pre-parturition.

Like wine, steak is in France a basic element, nationalized even more than socialized. It figures in all the surroundings of alimentary life: flat, edged with yellow, like the sole of a shoe, in cheap restaurants; thick and juicy in the bistros which specialize in it; cubic, with the core all moist throughout beneath a light charred crust, in haute cuisine. It is a part of all the rhythms, that of the comfortable bourgeois meal and that of the bachelor's bohemian snack. It is a food at once expeditious and dense, it effects the best possible ratio between economy and efficacy, between mythology and its multifarious ways of being consumed.

Moreover, it is a French possession (circumscribed today, it is true, by the invasion of American steaks). As in the case of wine there is no alimentary constraint which does not make the Frenchman dream of steak. Hardly abroad, he feels nostalgia for it. Steak is here adorned with a supplementary virtue of elegance, for among the apparent complexity of exotic cooking, it is a food which unites, one feels, succulence and simplicity. Being part of the nation, it follows the index of patriotic values: it helps them to rise in wartime, it is the very flesh of the French soldier, the inalienable property which cannot go over to the enemy except by treason. In an old film (*Deuxième Bureau contre Kommandantur*), the maid of the patriotic *curé* gives food to the Boche spy disguised as a French underground fighter: '*Ah, it's you, Laurent! I'll give you some steak.*' And then, when the spy is unmasked: '*And when I think I gave him some of my steak!*' — the supreme breach of trust.

Commonly associated with chips, steak communicates its national glamour to them: chips are nostalgic and patriotic like steak. *Match* told us that after the armistice in Indo-China '*General de Castries, for his first meal, asked for chips*'. And the President of the Indo-China Veterans, later commenting on this information added: '*The gesture of General de Castries asking for chips for his first meal has not always been understood.*' What we were meant to understand is that the General's request was certainly not a vulgar materialistic reflex, but an episode in the ritual of appropriating the regained French community. The General understood well our national symbolism; he knew that *la frite*, chips, are the alimentary sign of Frenchness.

The *Nautilus* and the Drunken Boat

The work of Jules Verne (whose centenary was recently celebrated) would be a good subject for a structural study: it is highly thematic. Verne has built a kind of self-sufficient cosmogony, which has its own categories, its own time, space, fulfilment and even existential principle.

This principle, it seems to me, is the ceaseless action of secluding oneself. Imagination about travel corresponds in Verne to an exploration of closure, and the compatibility between Verne and childhood does not stem from a banal mystique of adventure, but on the contrary from a common delight in the finite, which one also finds in children's passion for huts and tents: to enclose oneself and to settle, such is the existential dream of childhood and of Verne. The archetype of this dream is this almost perfect novel: *L'Ile mystérieuse*, in which the man-child re-invents the world, fills it, closes it, shuts himself up in it, and crowns this encyclopaedic effort with the bourgeois posture of appropriation: slippers, pipe and fireside, while outside the storm, that is, the infinite, rages in vain.

Verne had an obsession for plenitude: he never stopped putting a last touch to the world and furnishing it, making it full with an egg-like fullness. His tendency is exactly that of an eighteenth-century encyclopaedist or of a Dutch painter: the world is finite, the world is full of numerable and contiguous objects. The artist can have no other task than to make catalogues, inventories, and to watch out for small unfilled corners in order to conjure up there, in close ranks, the creations and the instruments of man. Verne belongs to the progressive lineage of the bourgeoisie: his work proclaims that nothing can escape man, that the world, even its most distant part, is like an object in his hand, and that, all told, property is but a dialectical moment in the general enslavement of Nature. Verne in no way sought to enlarge the world by romantic ways of escape or mystical plans to reach the infinite:

he constantly sought to shrink it, to populate it, to reduce it to a known and enclosed space, where man could subsequently live in comfort: the world can draw everything from itself; it needs, in order to exist, no one else but man.

Beyond the innumerable resources of science, Verne invented an excellent novelistic device in order to make more vivid this appropriation of the world: to pledge space by means of time, constantly to unite these two categories, to stake them on a single throw of the dice or a single impulse, which always come off. Even vicissitudes have the function of conferring on the world a sort of elastic state, making its limits more distant, then closer, blithely playing with cosmic distances, and mischievously testing the power of man over space and schedules. And on this planet which is triumphantly eaten by the Vernian hero, like a sort of bourgeois Antaeus whose nights are innocent and 'restoring', there often loiters some desperado, a prey to remorse and spleen, a relic from an extinct Romantic age, who strikingly shows up by contrast the health of the true owners of the world, who have no other concern but to adapt as perfectly as possible to situations whose complexity, in no way metaphysical nor even ethical, quite simply springs from some provocative whim of geography.

The basic activity in Jules Verne, then, is unquestionably that of appropriation. The image of the ship, so important in his mythology, in no way contradicts this. Quite the contrary: the ship may well be a symbol for departure; it is, at a deeper level, the emblem of closure. An inclination for ships always means the joy of perfectly enclosing oneself, of having at hand the greatest possible number of objects, and having at one's disposal an absolutely finite space. To like ships is first and foremost to like a house, a superlative one since it is unremittingly closed, and not at all vague sailings into the unknown: a ship is a habitat before being a means of transport. And sure enough, all the ships in Jules Verne are perfect cubby-holes, and the vastness of their circumnavigation further increases the bliss of their closure, the perfection of their inner humanity. The *Nautilus*, in this regard, is the most desirable of all caves: the enjoyment of being enclosed reaches its paroxysm when, from the bosom of this unbroken inwardness, it is possible to watch, through a large window-pane, the outside vagueness of the waters, and thus define, in a single act, the inside by means of its opposite.

Most ships in legend or fiction are, from this point of view, like the *Nautilus*, the theme of a cherished seclusion, for it is enough to present the ship as the habitat of man, for man immediately to organize there the enjoyment of a round, smooth universe, of which, in addition, a whole nautical morality makes him at once the god, the master and the owner (*sole master on board*, etc.). In this mythology of seafaring, there is only one means to exorcize the possessive nature of the man on a ship; it is to eliminate the man and to leave the ship on its own. The ship then is no longer a box, a habitat, an object that is owned; it becomes a travelling eye, which comes close to the infinite; it constantly begets departures. The object that is the true opposite of Verne's *Nautilus* is Rimbaud's *Drunken Boat*, the boat which says 'I' and, freed from its concavity, can make man proceed from a psycho-analysis of the cave to a genuine poetics of exploration.

The Brain of Einstein

Einstein's brain is a mythical object: paradoxically, the greatest intelligence of all provides an image of the most up-to-date machine, the man who is too powerful is removed from psychology, and introduced into a world of robots; as is well known, the supermen of science-fiction always have something reified about them. So has Einstein: he is commonly signified by his brain, which is like an object for anthologies, a true museum exhibit. Perhaps because of his mathematical specialization, superman is here divested of every magical character; no diffuse power in him, no mystery other than mechanical: he is a superior, a prodigious organ, but a real, even a physiological one. Mythologically, Einstein is matter, his power does not spontaneously draw one towards the spiritual, it needs the help of an independent morality, a reminder about the scientist's 'conscience' (*Science without conscience*,* they said …).

Einstein himself has to some extent been a party to the legend by bequeathing his brain, for the possession of which two hospitals are still fighting as if it were an unusual piece of machinery which it will at last be possible to dismantle. A photograph shows him lying down, his head bristling with electric wires: the waves of his brain are being recorded, while he is requested to 'think of relativity'. (But for that matter, what does 'to think of' mean, exactly?) What this is meant to convey is probably that the seismograms will be all the more violent since 'relativity' is an arduous subject. Thought itself is thus represented as an energetic material, the measurable product of a complex (quasi-electrical) apparatus which transforms cerebral substance into power. The mythology of Einstein shows him as a genius so lacking in magic that one speaks about his thought as of a functional labour analogous to the mechanical making of sausages, the grinding of

* 'Science without conscience is but the ruin of the Soul' (Rabelais, *Pantagruel* II, ch. 8).

corn or the crushing of ore: he used to produce thought, continuously, as a mill makes flour, and death was above all, for him, the cessation of a localized function: '*the most powerful brain of all has stopped thinking*'.

What this machine of genius was supposed to produce was equations. Through the mythology of Einstein, the world blissfully regained the image of knowledge reduced to a formula. Paradoxically, the more the genius of the man was materialized under the guise of his brain, the more the product of his inventiveness came to acquire a magical dimension, and gave a new incarnation to the old esoteric image of a science entirely contained in a few letters. There is a single secret to the world, and this secret is held in one word; the universe is a safe of which humanity seeks the combination: Einstein almost found it, this is the myth of Einstein. In it, we find all the Gnostic themes: the unity of nature, the ideal possibility of a fundamental reduction of the world, the unfastening power of the word, the age-old struggle between a secret and an utterance, the idea that total knowledge can only be discovered all at once, like a lock which suddenly opens after a thousand unsuccessful attempts. The historic equation $E = mc^2$, by its unexpected simplicity, almost embodies the pure idea of the key, bare, linear, made of one metal, opening with a wholly magical ease a door which had resisted the desperate efforts of centuries. Popular imagery faithfully expresses this: *photographs* of Einstein show him standing next to a blackboard covered with mathematical signs of obvious complexity; but *cartoons* of Einstein (the sign that he has become a legend) show him chalk still in hand, and having just written on an empty blackboard, as if without preparation, the magic formula of the world. In this way mythology shows an awareness of the nature of the various tasks: research proper brings into play clockwork-like mechanisms and has its seat in a wholly material organ which is monstrous only by its cybernetic complication; discovery, on the contrary, has a magical essence, it is simple like a basic element, a principial substance, like the philosophers' stone of hermetists, tar-water for Berkeley, or oxygen for Schelling.

But since the world is still going on, since research is proliferating, and on the other hand since God's share must be preserved, some failure on the part of Einstein is necessary: Einstein died, it is said, without having been able to verify *'the equation in which the secret of the world was enclosed'*. So in the end the world resisted; hardly opened, the secret closed again, the code was incomplete. In this way Einstein fulfils all the conditions of myth, which could not care less about contradictions so long as it establishes a euphoric security: at once magician and machine, eternal researcher and unfulfilled discoverer, unleashing the best and the worst, brain and conscience, Einstein embodies the most contradictory dreams, and mythically reconciles the infinite power of man over nature with the 'fatality' of the sacrosanct, which man cannot yet do without.

The Jet-man

The *jet-man* is a jet-pilot. *Match* has specified that he belongs to a new race in aviation, nearer to the robot than to the hero. Yet there are in the *jet-man* several Parsifalian residues, as we shall see shortly. But what strikes one first in the mythology of the *jet-man* is the elimination of speed: nothing in the legend alludes to this experience. We must here accept a paradox, which is in fact admitted by everyone with the greatest of ease, and even consumed as a proof of modernity. This paradox is that an excess of speed turns into repose. The pilot-hero was made unique by a whole mythology of speed as an experience, of space devoured, of intoxicating motion; the *jet-man*, on the other hand, is defined by a coenaesthesis of motionlessness ('*at 2,000 km per hour, in level flight, no impression of speed at all*'), as if the extravagance of his vocation precisely consisted in *overtaking* motion, in going faster than speed. Mythology abandons here a whole imagery of exterior friction and enters pure coenaesthesis: motion is no longer the optical perception of points and surfaces; it has become a kind of vertical disorder, made of contractions, black-outs, terrors and faints; it is no longer a gliding but an inner devastation, an unnatural perturbation, a motionless crisis of bodily consciousness.

No wonder if, carried to such a pitch, the myth of the aviator loses all humanism. The hero of classical speed could remain a 'gentleman', inasmuch as motion was for him an occasional exploit, for which courage alone was required: one went faster in bursts, like a daring amateur, not like a professional, one sought an 'intoxication', one came to motion equipped with an age-old moralizing which made its perception keener and enabled one to express its philosophy. It is inasmuch as speed was an *adventure* that it linked the airman to a whole series of human roles.

The *jet-man*, on the other hand, no longer seems to know either adventure or destiny, but only a condition. Yet this condition is at first sight less human than anthropological: mythically, the *jet-man* is defined less by his courage than by his weight, his diet and his habits (temperance, frugality, continence). His racial apartness can be read in his morphology: the anti-G suit of inflatable nylon, the shiny helmet, introduce the *jet-man* into a novel type of skin in which *'even his mother would not know him'*. We are dealing with a true racial conversion, all the more credible since science-fiction has already largely substantiated this metamorphosis of species: everything happens as if there had been a sudden mutation between the earlier creatures of propeller-mankind and the later ones of jet-mankind.

In fact, and in spite of the scientific garb of this new mythology, there has merely been a displacement of the sacred: after the hagiographic era (Saints and Martyrs of propeller-aviation) there follows a monastic period; and what passes at first for mere dietetic prescriptions soon appears invested with a sacerdotal significance: continence and temperance, abstention and withdrawal from pleasures, community life, uniform clothing — everything concurs, in the mythology of the *jet-man*, to make manifest the plasticity of the flesh, its submission to collective ends (chastely undefined, by the way), and it is this submission which is offered as a sacrifice to the glamorous singularity of an inhuman condition. Society eventually recognizes, à propos of the *jet-man*, the old theosophical pact, which has always compensated power by an ascetic life, paid for semi-divinity in the coin of human 'happiness'. So truly does the situation of the *jet-man* comprise the sense of a religious call, that it is itself the reward of previous austerities, of initiatory proceedings, meant to test the postulant (passage through the altitude chamber and in the centrifugal machine). Right down to the Instructor, greying, anonymous and inscrutable, who is perfectly suited to the part of the necessary mystagogue. As for endurance, we are definitely told that, as is the case in all initiations, it is not physical in nature: triumph in preliminary ordeals is, truth to tell, the fruit of a spiritual gift, one is gifted for jet-flying as others are called to God.

All this would be commonplace if we were dealing with the traditional hero, whose whole value was to fly without forgoing his humanity (like Saint-Exupéry who was a writer, or Lindbergh who flew in a lounge-suit). But the mythological peculiarity of the *jet-man* is that he keeps none of the romantic and individualistic elements of the sacred role, without nevertheless forsaking the role itself. Assimilated by his name to pure passivity (what is more inert and more dispossessed than an object *expelled in jet-form*?), he reintegrates the ritual nevertheless, thanks to the myth of a fictitious, celestial race, which is said to derive its peculiarities from its ascetic life, and which effects a kind of anthropological compromise between humans and Martians. The *jet-man* is a reified hero, as if even today men could conceive the heavens only as populated with semi-objects.

The *Blue Guide*

The *Blue Guide** hardly knows the existence of scenery except under the guise of the picturesque. The picturesque is found any time the ground is uneven. We find again here this bourgeois promoting of the mountains, this old Alpine myth (since it dates back to the nineteenth century) which Gide rightly associated with Helvetico-Protestant morality and which has always functioned as a hybrid compound of the cult of nature and of puritanism (regeneration through clean air, moral ideas at the sight of mountain-tops, summit-climbing as civic virtue, etc.). Among the views elevated by the *Blue Guide* to aesthetic existence, we rarely find plains (redeemed only when they can be described as fertile), never plateaux. Only mountains, gorges, defiles and torrents can have access to the pantheon of travel, inasmuch, probably, as they seem to encourage a morality of effort and solitude. Travel according to the *Blue Guide* is thus revealed as a labour-saving adjustment, the easy substitute for the morally uplifting walk. This in itself means that the mythology of the *Blue Guide* dates back to the last century, to that phase in history when the bourgeoisie was enjoying a kind of new-born euphoria in *buying* effort, in keeping its image and essence without feeling any of its ill-effects. It is therefore in the last analysis, quite logically and quite stupidly, the gracelessness of a landscape, its lack of spaciousness or human appeal, its verticality, so contrary to the bliss of travel, which account for its interest. Ultimately, the *Guide* will coolly write: *'The road becomes very picturesque (tunnels)'*: it matters little that one no longer sees anything, since the tunnel here has become the sufficient sign of the mountain; it is a financial security stable enough for one to have no further worry about its value over the counter.

Just as hilliness is overstressed to such an extent as to eliminate all other types of scenery, the human life of a country disappears

* Hachette World Guides, dubbed 'Guide Bleu' in French.

to the exclusive benefit of its monuments. For the *Blue Guide*, men exist only as 'types'. In Spain, for instance, the Basque is an adventurous sailor, the Levantine a light-hearted gardener, the Catalan a clever tradesman and the Cantabrian a sentimental highlander. We find again here this disease of thinking in essences, which is at the bottom of every bourgeois mythology of man (which is why we come across it so often). The ethnic reality of Spain is thus reduced to a vast classical ballet, a nice neat commedia dell'arte, whose improbable typology serves to mask the real spectacle of conditions, classes and professions. For the *Blue Guide*, men exist as social entities only in trains, where they fill a 'very mixed' Third Class. Apart from that, they are a mere introduction, they constitute a charming and fanciful decor, meant to surround the essential part of the country: its collection of monuments.

If one excepts its wild defiles, fit for moral ejaculations, Spain according to the *Blue Guide* knows only one type of space, that which weaves, across a few nondescript lacunae, a close web of churches, vestries, reredoses, crosses, altar-curtains, spires (always octagonal), sculpted groups (Family and Labour), Romanesque porches, naves and life-size crucifixes. It can be seen that all these monuments are religious, for from a bourgeois point of view it is almost impossible to conceive a History of Art which is not Christian and Roman Catholic. Christianity is the chief purveyor of tourism, and one travels only to visit churches. In the case of Spain, this imperialism is ludicrous, for Catholicism often appears there as a barbaric force which has stupidly defaced the earlier achievements of Muslim civilization: the mosque at Cordoba, whose wonderful forest of columns is at every turn obstructed by massive blocks of altars, or a colossal Virgin (set up by Franco) denaturing the site which it aggressively dominates — all this should help the French bourgeois to glimpse at least once in his life that historically there is also a reverse side to Christianity.

Generally speaking, the *Blue Guide* testifies to the futility of all analytical descriptions, those which reject both explanations and phenomenology: it answers in fact none of the questions which a modern traveller can ask himself while crossing a countryside which is real *and which exists in time*. To select only monuments suppresses at one stroke the reality of the land and that of its people, it accounts for nothing of the present, that is, nothing historical, and as a consequence, the monuments themselves become undecipherable, therefore senseless. What is to be seen is thus constantly in the process of vanishing, and the *Guide* becomes, through an operation common to all mystifications, the very opposite of what it advertises, an agent of blindness. By reducing geography to the description of an uninhabited world of monuments, the *Blue Guide* expresses a mythology which is obsolete for a part of the bourgeoisie itself. It is unquestionable that travel has become (or become again) a method of approach based on human realities rather than 'culture': once again (as in the eighteenth century, perhaps) it is everyday life which is the main object of travel, and it is social geography, town-planning, sociology, economics which outline the framework of the actual questions asked today even by the merest layman. But as for the *Blue Guide*, it still abides by a partly superseded bourgeois mythology, that which postulated (religious) Art as the fundamental value of culture, but saw its 'riches' and 'treasures' only as a reassuring accumulation of goods (cf. the creation of museums). This behaviour expressed a double urge: to have at one's disposal a cultural alibi as ethereal as possible, and to maintain this alibi in the toils of a computable and acquisitive system, so that one could at any moment do the accounts of the ineffable. It goes without saying that this myth of travel is becoming quite anachronistic, even among the bourgeoisie, and I suppose that if one entrusted the preparation of a new guide-book to, say, the lady-editors at *L'Express* or the editors of *Match*, we would see appearing, questionable as they would still probably be, quite different countries: after the Spain of Anquetil or Larousse, would follow the Spain of Siegfried, then that of Fourastié. Notice how already, in the *Michelin Guide*, the number of bathrooms and forks indicating good restaurants is vying with that of 'artistic curiosities': even bourgeois myths have their differential geology.

It is true that in the case of Spain, the blinkered and old-fashioned character of the description is what is best suited to the latent support given by the *Guide* to Franco. Beside the historical accounts proper (which are rare and meagre, incidentally, for it is well known that History is not a good bourgeois), those accounts in which the Republicans are always '*extremists*' looting churches — but nothing on Guernica — while the good 'Nationalists', on the contrary, spend their time '*liberating*', solely by '*skilful strategic manoeuvres*' and '*heroic feats of resistance*', let me mention the flowering of a splendid myth-alibi: that of the *prosperity* of the country. Needless to say, this prosperity is 'statistical' and 'global', or to be more accurate: 'commercial'. The *Guide* does not tell us, of course, how this fine prosperity is shared out: *hierarchically*, probably, since they think it fit to tell us that '*the serious and patient effort of this people has also included the reform of its political system, in order to achieve regeneration through the loyal application of sound principles of order and hierarchy.*'

Ornamental Cookery

The weekly *Elle* (a real mythological treasure) gives us almost every week a fine colour photograph of a prepared dish: golden partridges studded with cherries, a faintly pink chicken chaud-froid, a mould of crayfish surrounded by their red shells, a frothy charlotte prettified with glacé fruit designs, multicoloured trifle, etc.

The 'substantial' category which prevails in this type of cooking is that of the smooth coating: there is an obvious endeavour to glaze surfaces, to round them off, to bury the food under the even sediment of sauces, creams, icing and jellies. This of course comes from the very finality of the coating, which belongs to a visual category, and cooking according to *Elle* is meant for the eye alone, since sight is a genteel sense. For there is, in this persistence of glazing, a need for gentility. *Elle* is a highly valuable journal, from the point of view of legend at least, since its role is to present to its vast public which (market-research tells us) is working-class, the very dream of smartness. Hence a cookery which is based on coatings and alibis, and is for ever trying to extenuate and even to disguise the primary nature of foodstuffs, the brutality of meat or the abruptness of sea-food. A country dish is admitted only as an exception (the good family boiled beef), as the rustic whim of jaded city-dwellers.

But above all, coatings prepare and support one of the major developments of genteel cookery: ornamentation. Glazing, in *Elle*, serves as background for unbridled beautification: chiselled mushrooms, punctuation of cherries, motifs of carved lemon, shavings of truffle, silver pastilles, arabesques of glacé fruit: the underlying coat (and this is why I called it a sediment, since the food itself becomes no more than an indeterminate bed-rock) is intended to be the page on which can be read a whole rococo cookery (there is a partiality for a pinkish colour).

Ornamentation proceeds in two contradictory ways, which we shall in a moment see dialectically reconciled: on the one hand, fleeing from nature thanks to a kind of frenzied baroque (sticking shrimps in a lemon, making a chicken look pink, serving grapefruit hot), and on the other, trying to reconstitute it through an incongruous artifice (strewing meringue mushrooms and holly leaves on a traditional log-shaped Christmas cake, replacing the heads of crayfish around the sophisticated bechamel which hides their bodies). It is in fact the same pattern which one finds in the elaboration of petit-bourgeois trinkets (ashtrays in the shape of a saddle, lighters in the shape of a cigarette, terrines in the shape of a hare).

This is because here, as in all petit-bourgeois art, the irrepressible tendency towards extreme realism is countered – or balanced – by one of the eternal imperatives of journalism for women's magazines: what is pompously called, at *L'Express*, *having ideas*. Cookery in *Elle* is, in the same way, an 'idea'-cookery. But here inventiveness, confined to a fairy-land reality, must be applied only to *garnishings*, for the genteel tendency of the magazine precludes it from touching on the real problems concerning food (the real problem is not to have the idea of sticking cherries into a partridge, it is to have the partridge, that is to say, to pay for it).

This ornamental cookery is indeed supported by wholly mythical economics. This is an openly dream-like cookery, as proved in fact by the photographs in *Elle*, which never show the dishes except from a high angle, as objects at once near and inaccessible, whose consumption can perfectly well be accomplished simply by looking. It is, in the fullest meaning of the word, a cuisine of advertisement, totally magical, especially when one remembers that this magazine is widely read in small-income groups. The latter, in fact, explains the former: it is because *Elle* is addressed to a genuinely working-class public that it is very careful not to take for granted that cooking must be economical. Compare with *L'Express*, whose exclusively middle-class public enjoys a comfortable purchasing power: its cookery is real, not

79

magical. *Elle* gives the recipe of fancy partridges, *L'Express* gives that of *salade niçoise*. The readers of *Elle* are entitled only to fiction; one can suggest real dishes to those of *L'Express*, in the certainty that they will be able to prepare them. ·

Neither-Nor Criticism

We were able to read in one of the first numbers of *L'Express* (the daily) the (anonymous) profession of faith of a critic, which was a superb piece of balanced rhetoric. Its idea was that criticism must be *'neither a parlour game, nor a municipal service'* — which means that it must be neither reactionary nor communist, neither gratuitous nor political.

We are dealing here with a mechanism based on a double exclusion largely pertaining to this enumerative mania which we have already come across several times, and which I thought I could broadly define as a petit-bourgeois trait. One reckons all the methods with scales, one piles them up on each side as one thinks best, so as to appear oneself as an imponderable arbiter endowed with a spirituality which is ideal and thereby *just*, like the beam which is the judge in the weighing.

The faults indispensable to this operation of accountancy consist in the morality of the terms used. According to an old terrorist device (one cannot escape terrorism at will), one judges at the same time as one names, and the word, ballasted by a prior culpability, quite naturally comes to weigh down one of the scales. For instance, *culture* will be opposed to *ideologies*. Culture is a noble, universal thing, placed outside social choices: culture has no weight. Ideologies, on the other hand, are partisan inventions: so, onto the scales, and out with them! Both sides are dismissed under the stern gaze of culture (without realizing that culture itself is, in the last analysis, an ideology). Everything happens as if there were on one side heavy, defective words (*ideology, catechism, militant*), meant to serve for the ignominious game of the scales; and on the other, light, pure, immaterial words, noble by divine right, sublime to the point of evading the sordid law of numbers (*adventure, passion, grandeur, vir   'onour*), words placed above the sorry computation of lies. The latter group has the function of admonishing the former: there are words which are criminal and there are others which judge them. Needless to say, this fine morality of the Third Party unavoidably leads to new dichotomy, quite as simplistic as that which one wanted to expose in the very name of complexity. True, our world may well be subjected to a law of alternations; but you can be sure that it is a schism without Tribunal; no salvation for the judges: they also are well and truly committed.

Besides, it is enough to see which other myths emerge in this *Neither-Nor* criticism, to understand on which side it is situated. Without speaking further on the myth of timelessness which is at the core of any appeal to an eternal 'culture' ('*an art for all time*'), I also find, in our *Neither-Nor* doctrine, two common expedients of bourgeois mythology. The first consists in a certain idea of freedom, conceived as '*the refusal of* a priori *judgments*'. Now a literary judgment is always determined by the whole of which it is a part, and the very absence of a system — especially when it becomes a profession of faith — stems from a very definite system, which in this case is a very common variety of bourgeois ideology (or of culture, as our anonymous writer would say). It can even be said it is when man proclaims his primal liberty that his subordination is least disputable. One can without fear defy anyone ever to practise an innocent criticism, free from any systematic determination: the *Neither-Nor* brigade themselves are committed to a system, which is not necessarily the one to which they proclaim their allegiance. One cannot judge Literature without some previous idea of Man and History, of Good, Evil, Society, etc.: even in the simple word *adventure*, which is used with such alacrity by our *Neither-Nor* critics in order to moralize against those nasty systems which '*don't cause any surprise*', what heredity, what fatality, what routine! Any kind of freedom always in the end re-integrates a known type of coherence, which is nothing but a given *a priori*. So that freedom, for the critic, is not to refuse the wager (impossible!), it is to make his own wager obvious or not.*

The second bourgeois symptom in our text is the euphoric reference to the 'style' of the writer as to an eternal value of

* An allusion to Pascal's wager.

Literature. And yet, nothing can escape being put into question by History; not even *good writing*. Style is quite precisely dated as a critical value, and to make claims in the name of 'style' at the very time when some important writers have attacked this last stronghold in the mythology of classicism, is to show thereby a certain archaism: no, to come back once more to 'style' is not adventure! Better advised in a subsequent number, *L'Express* published a pertinent protest by A. Robbe-Grillet against the magical appeal to Stendhal ('*it reads just like Stendhal*'). A certain union of style and humanity (as in Anatole France, for instance) is perhaps no longer sufficient as a basis for 'Literature'. It is even to be feared that 'style', compromised by so many falsely human works, has finally become something suspect *a priori*: it is, at any rate, a value which should only be put to the credit of the writer awaiting a proper appraisal. This does not mean, naturally, that Literature can exist without some formal artifice. But, with due respect to our *Neither-Nor* critics, who are invariably the adepts of a bi-partite universe where they would represent divine transcendence, the opposite of *good writing* is not necessarily *bad writing*: today it is perhaps just *writing*. Literature has entered a situation which is difficult, restricted, mortal. It is no longer its ornaments that it is defending, but its skin: I rather fear that the new *Neither-Nor* criticism is one season behind.

Striptease

Striptease — at least Parisian striptease — is based on a contradiction: Woman is desexualized at the very moment when she is stripped naked. We may therefore say that we are dealing in a sense with a spectacle based on fear, or rather on the pretence of fear, as if eroticism here went no further than a sort of delicious terror, whose ritual signs have only to be announced to evoke at once the idea of sex and its conjuration.

It is only the time taken in shedding clothes which makes voyeurs of the public; but here, as in any mystifying spectacle, the decor, the props and the stereotypes intervene to contradict the initially provocative intention and eventually bury it in insignificance: evil is *advertised* the better to impede and exorcize it. French striptease seems to stem from what I have earlier called 'Operation Margarine', a mystifying device which consists in inoculating the public with a touch of evil, the better to plunge it afterwards into a permanently immune Moral Good: a few particles of eroticism, highlighted by the very situation on which the show is based, are in fact absorbed in a reassuring ritual which negates the flesh as surely as the vaccine or the taboo circumscribe and control the illness or the crime.

There will therefore be in striptease a whole series of coverings placed upon the body of the woman in proportion as she pretends to strip it bare. Exoticism is the first of these barriers, for it is always of a petrified kind which transports the body into the world of legend or romance: a Chinese woman equipped with an opium pipe (the indispensable symbol of 'Sininess'*), an undulating vamp with a gigantic cigarette-holder, a Venetian decor complete with gondola, a dress with panniers and a singer of serenades: all aim at establishing the woman *right from the start* as an object in disguise. The end of the striptease is then no longer to drag into the light a hidden depth, but to signify,

* See below, p. 121.

through the shedding of an incongruous and artificial clothing, nakedness as a *natural* vesture of woman, which amounts in the end to regaining a perfectly chaste state of the flesh.

The classic props of the music-hall, which are invariably rounded up here, constantly make the unveiled body more remote, and force it back into the all-pervading ease of a well-known rite: the furs, the fans, the gloves, the feathers, the fish-net stockings, in short the whole spectrum of adornment, constantly makes the living body return to the category of luxurious objects which surround man with a magical decor. Covered with feathers or gloved, the woman identifies herself here as a stereotyped element of music-hall, and to shed objects as ritualistic as these is no longer a part of a further, genuine un-dressing. Feathers, furs and gloves go on pervading the woman with their magical virtue even once removed, and give her something like the enveloping memory of a luxurious shell, for it is a self-evident law that the whole of striptease is given in the very nature of the initial garment: if the latter is improbable, as in the case of the Chinese woman or the woman in furs, the nakedness which follows remains itself unreal, smooth and enclosed like a beautiful slippery object, withdrawn by its very extravagance from human use: this is the underlying significance of the G-String covered with diamonds or sequins which is the very end of striptease. This ultimate triangle, by its pure and geometrical shape, by its hard and shiny material, bars the way to the sexual parts like a sword of purity, and definitively drives the woman back into a mineral world, the (precious) stone being here the irrefutable symbol of the absolute object, that which serves no purpose.

Contrary to the common prejudice, the dance which accom-panies the striptease from beginning to end is in no way an erotic element. It is probably quite the reverse: the faintly rhythmical undulation in this case exorcizes the fear of immobility. Not only does it give to the show the alibi of Art (the dances in strip-shows are always 'artistic'), but above all it constitutes the last barrier, and the most efficient of all: the dance, consisting of ritual gestures which have been seen a thousand times, acts on movements as a cosmetic, it hides nudity, and smothers the spectacle under a glaze of superfluous yet essential gestures, for the act of becoming bare is here relegated to the rank of parasitical operations carried out in an improbable background. Thus we see the professionals of striptease wrap themselves in the miraculous ease which constantly clothes them, makes them remote, gives them the icy indifference of skilful practitioners, haughtily taking refuge in the sureness of their technique: their science clothes them like a garment.

All this, this meticulous exorcism of sex, can be verified *a contrario* in the 'popular contests' (*sic*) of amateur striptease: there, 'beginners' undress in front of a few hundred spectators without resorting or resorting very clumsily to magic, which unquestionably restores to the spectacle its erotic power. Here we find at the beginning far fewer Chinese or Spanish women, no feathers or furs (sensible suits, ordinary coats), few disguises as a starting point—gauche steps, unsatisfactory dancing, girls constantly threatened by immobility, and above all by a 'technical' awkwardness (the resistance of briefs, dress or bra) which gives to the gestures of unveiling an unexpected importance, denying the woman the alibi of art and the refuge of being an object, imprisoning her in a condition of weakness and timorousness.

And yet, at the *Moulin Rouge*, we see hints of another kind of exorcism, probably typically French, and one which in actual fact tends less to nullify eroticism than to tame it: the compère tries to give striptease a reassuring petit-bourgeois status. To start with, striptease is a *sport*: there is a Striptease Club, which organizes healthy contests whose winners come out crowned and rewarded with edifying prizes (a subscription to physical training lessons), a novel (which can only be Robbe-Grillet's *Voyeur*), or useful prizes (a pair of nylons, five thousand francs). Then, striptease is identified with a *career* (beginners, semi-professionals, professionals), that is, to the honourable practice of a specialization (strippers are skilled workers). One can even give them the magical alibi of work: *vocation*; one girl is, say, '*doing well*' or '*well on the way to fulfilling her promise*', or on the contrary '*taking her first steps*' on the arduous path of striptease. Finally and above all, the competitors are socially situated: one is a salesgirl, another a secretary (there are many secretaries in the Striptease Club). Striptease here is made to rejoin the world of the public, is made familiar and bourgeois, as if the French, unlike the American public (at least according to what one hears), following an irresistible tendency of their social status, could not conceive eroticism except as a household property, sanctioned by the alibi of weekly sport much more than by that of a magical spectacle: and this is how, in France, striptease is nationalized.

The New Citroën

I think that cars today are almost the exact equivalent of the great Gothic cathedrals: I mean the supreme creation of an era, conceived with passion by unknown artists, and consumed in image if not in usage by a whole population which appropriates them as a purely magical object.

It is obvious that the new Citroën has fallen from the sky inasmuch as it appears at first sight as a superlative *object*. We must not forget that an object is the best messenger of a world above that of nature: one can easily see in an object at once a perfection and an absence of origin, a closure and a brilliance, a transformation of life into matter (matter is much more magical than life), and in a word a *silence* which belongs to the realm of fairy-tales. The *D.S.* — the 'Goddess' — has all the features (or at least the public is unanimous in attributing them to it at first sight) of one of those objects from another universe which have supplied fuel for the neomania of the eighteenth century and that of our own science-fiction: the *Déesse* is *first and foremost* a new *Nautilus*.

This is why it excites interest less by its substance than by the junction of its components. It is well known that smoothness is always an attribute of perfection because its opposite reveals a technical and typically human operation of assembling: Christ's robe was seamless, just as the airships of science-fiction are made of unbroken metal. The *D.S. 19* has no pretensions about being as smooth as cake-icing, although its general shape is very rounded; yet it is the dove-tailing of its sections which interest the public most: one keenly fingers the edges of the windows, one feels along the wide rubber grooves which link the back window to its metal surround. There are in the *D.S.* the beginnings of a new phenomenology of assembling, as if one progressed from a world where elements are welded to a world where they are juxtaposed and hold together by sole virtue of their wondrous shape, which of course is meant to prepare one for the idea of a more benign Nature.

As for the material itself, it is certain that it promotes a taste for lightness in its magical sense. There is a return to a certain degree of streamlining, new, however, since it is less bulky, less incisive, more relaxed than that which one found in the first period of this fashion. Speed here is expressed by less aggressive, less athletic signs, as if it were evolving from a primitive to a classical form. This spiritualization can be seen in the extent, the quality and the material of the glass-work. The *Déesse* is obviously the exaltation of glass, and pressed metal is only a support for it. Here, the glass surfaces are not windows, openings pierced in a dark shell; they are vast walls of air and space, with the curvature, the spread and the brilliance of soap-bubbles, the hard thinness of a substance more entomological than mineral (the Citroën emblem, with its arrows, has in fact become a winged emblem, as if one was proceeding from the category of propulsion to that of spontaneous motion, from that of the engine to that of the organism).

We are therefore dealing here with a humanized art, and it is possible that the *Déesse* marks a change in the mythology of cars. Until now, the ultimate in cars belonged rather to the bestiary of power; here it becomes at once more spiritual and more object-like, and despite some concessions to neomania (such as the empty steering wheel), it is now more *homely*, more attuned to this sublimation of the utensil which one also finds in the design of contemporary household equipment. The dashboard looks more like the working surface of a modern kitchen than the control-room of a factory: the slim panes of matt fluted metal, the small levers topped by a white ball, the very simple dials, the very discreteness of the nickel-work, all this signifies a kind of control exercised over motion, which is henceforth conceived as comfort rather than performance. One is obviously turning from an alchemy of speed to a relish in driving.

The public, it seems, has admirably divined the novelty of the themes which are suggested to it. Responding at first to the neologism (a whole publicity campaign had kept it on the alert for years), it tries very quickly to fall back on a behaviour which indicates adjustment and a readiness to use ('*You've got to get used to it*'). In the exhibition halls, the car on show is explored with an intense, amorous studiousness: it is the great tactile phase of discovery, the moment when visual wonder is about to receive the reasoned assault of touch (for touch is the most demystifying of all senses, unlike sight, which is the most magical). The bodywork, the lines of union are touched, the upholstery palpated, the seats tried, the doors caressed, the cushions fondled; before the wheel, one pretends to drive with one's whole body. The object here is totally prostituted, appropriated: originating from the heaven of *Metropolis*, the Goddess is in a quarter of an hour mediatized, actualizing through this exorcism the very essence of petit-bourgeois advancement.

Photography and Electoral Appeal

Some candidates for Parliament adorn their electoral prospectus with a portrait. This presupposes that photography has a power to convert which must be analysed. To start with, the effigy of a candidate establishes a personal link between him and the voters; the candidate does not only offer a programme for judgment, he suggests a physical climate, a set of daily choices expressed in a morphology, a way of dressing, a posture. Photography thus tends to restore the paternalistic nature of elections, whose elitist essence has been disrupted by proportional representation and the rule of parties (the Right seems to use it more than the Left). Inasmuch as photography is an ellipse of language and a condensation of an 'ineffable' social whole, it constitutes an anti-intellectual weapon and tends to spirit away 'politics' (that is to say a body of problems and solutions) to the advantage of a 'manner of being', a socio-moral status. It is well known that this antithesis is one of the major myths of Poujadism (Poujade on television saying: '*Look at me: I am like you*').

Electoral photography is therefore above all the acknowledgment of something deep and irrational co-extensive with politics. What is transmitted through the photograph of the candidate are not his plans, but his deep motives, all his family, mental, even erotic circumstances, all this style of life of which he is at once the product, the example and the bait. It is obvious that what most of our candidates offer us through their likeness is a type of social setting, the spectacular comfort of family, legal and religious norms, the suggestion of innately owning such items of bourgeois property as Sunday Mass, xenophobia, steak and chips, cuckold jokes, in short, what we call an ideology. Needless to say the use of electoral photography presupposes a kind of complicity: a photograph is a mirror, what we are asked to read is the familiar, the known; it offers to the voter his own likeness, but clarified, exalted, superbly elevated into a type. This glorification is in fact the very definition of the photogenic: the voter is at once expressed and heroized, he is invited to elect himself, to weigh the mandate which he is about to give with a veritable physical transference: he is delegating his 'race'.

The types which are thus delegated are not very varied. First there is that which stands for social status, respectability, whether sanguine and well-fed (lists of 'National' parties), or genteel and insipid (lists of the M.R.P. – the Christian Democrats). Then, the type of the intellectual (let it be repeated that we are dealing here with 'signified' types, not actual ones): whether sanctimonious like the candidate of centre right parties like the Rassemblement National, or 'searching' like that of the Communists. In the last two cases, the iconography is meant to signify the exceptional conjunction of thought and will, reflection and action: the slightly narrowed eyes allow a sharp look to filter through, which seems to find its strength in a beautiful inner dream without however ceasing to alight on real obstacles, as if the ideal candidate had in this case magnificently to unite social idealism with bourgeois empiricism. The last type is quite simply that of the 'good-looking chap', whose obvious credentials are his health and virility. Some candidates, incidentally, beautifully manage to win on both counts, appearing for instance as a handsome hero (in uniform) on one side of the handout, and as a mature and virile citizen on the other, displaying his little family. For in most cases, the morphological type is assisted by very obvious attributes: one candidate is surrounded by his kids (curled and dolled-up like all children photographed in France), another is a young parachutist with rolled-up sleeves, or an officer with his chest covered with decorations. Photography constitutes here a veritable blackmail by means of moral values: country, army, family, honour, reckless heroism.

The conventions of photography, moreover, are themselves replete with signs. A full-face photograph underlines the realistic outlook of the candidate, especially if he is provided with scrutinizing glasses. Everything there expresses penetration, gravity, frankness: the future deputy is looking squarely at the enemy, the obstacle, the 'problem'. A three-quarter face photograph, which is more common, suggests the tyranny of an ideal: the gaze is lost nobly in the future, it does not confront, it soars, and fertilizes some other domain, which is chastely left undefined. Almost all three-quarter face photos arc ascensional, the face is lifted towards a supernatural light which draws it up and elevates it to the realm of a higher humanity; the candidate reaches the Olympus of elevated feelings, where all political contradictions are solved: peace and war in Algeria, social progress and employers' profits, so-called 'free' religious schools and subsidies from the sugar-beet lobby, the Right and the Left (an opposition always 'superseded'!): all these coexist peacefully in this thoughtful gaze, nobly fixed on the hidden interests of Order.

The Lost Continent

A film, *The Lost Continent*, throws a clear light on the current myth of exoticism. It is a big documentary on 'the East', the pretext of which is some undefined ethnographic expedition, evidently false, incidentally, led by three or four bearded Italians into the Malay Archipelago. The film is euphoric, everything in it is easy, innocent. Our explorers are good fellows, who fill up their leisure time with child-like amusements: they play with their mascot, a little bear (a mascot is indispensable in all expeditions: no film about the polar region is without its tame seal, no documentary on the tropics is without its monkey), or they comically upset a dish of spaghetti on the deck. Which means that these good people, anthropologists though they are, don't bother much with historical or sociological problems. Penetrating the Orient never means more for them than a little trip in a boat, on an azure sea, in an essentially sunny country. And this same Orient which has today become the political centre of the world we see here all flattened, made smooth and gaudily coloured like an old-fashioned postcard.

The device which produces irresponsibility is clear: colouring the world is always a means of denying it (and perhaps one should at this point begin an inquiry into the use of colour in the cinema). Deprived of all substance, driven back into colour, disembodied through the very glamour of the 'images', the Orient is ready for the spiriting away which the film has in store for it. What with the bear as a mascot and the droll spaghetti, our studio anthropologists will have no trouble in postulating an Orient which is exotic in form, while being in reality profoundly similar to the Occident, at least the Occident of spiritualist thought. Orientals have religions of their own? Never mind, these variations matter very little compared to the basic unity of idealism. Every rite is thus made at once specific and eternal, promoted at one stroke into a piquant spectacle and a quasi-Christian symbol.

And even if Buddhism is not strictly speaking Christian, does it matter, since it also has nuns who have their heads shaven (a major theme in the pathos of all ceremonies of taking the veil), since it has monks who kneel and confess to their superior, and finally since, as in Seville, the faithful come and cover with gold the statue of their god?[1] It is true that it is always the forms which emphasize best the identity of all religions; but here this identity, far from unmasking them, gives them a firm basis instead and credits them all to a higher form of Catholicism.

It is well known that syncretism has always been one of the great assimilating techniques of the Church. In the seventeenth century, in this same Orient whose Christian predispositions are shown to us by *The Lost Continent*, the Jesuits went very far towards the oecumenicity of forms: thus were born the Malabar rites, which the Pope, in fact, eventually condemned. It is this same '*all things are alike*' which is hinted at by our ethnographers: East and West, it is all the same, they are only different in hue, their essential core is identical, and that is the eternal postulation of man towards God, the paltry and contingent character of geographical considerations compared to this human nature of which Christianity alone holds the key. Even the legends, all this 'primitive' folklore whose strangeness seems ostensibly pointed out to us, have as their sole mission the illustration of 'Nature': the rites, the cultural facts, are never related to a particular historical order, an explicit economic or social status, but only to the great neutral forms of cosmic commonplaces (the seasons, storms, death, etc.). If we are concerned with fishermen, it is not at all the type of fishing which is shown; but rather, drowned in a garish sunset and eternalized, a romantic essence of the fisherman, presented not as a workman dependent by his technique and his gains on a definite society, but rather as the theme of an eternal condition, in which man is far away and exposed to the perils of the sea, and woman weeping and praying at home. The same applies to refugees, a long procession of which

[1] This provides us with a fine example of the mystifying power of music: all the 'Buddhist' scenes are supported by a nondescript musical treacle, which takes after both American crooning and Gregorian chant: it is monodic, anyway (the sign of monasticity).

is shown at the beginning, coming down a mountain: to identify them is of course unnecessary: they are eternal essences of refugees, which it is in the *nature* of the East to produce.

· All told, exoticism here shows well its fundamental justification, which is to deny any identification by History. By appending to Eastern realities a few positive signs which mean 'native', one reliably immunizes them against any responsible content. A little 'situating', as superficial as possible, supplies the necessary alibi and exempts one from accounting for the situation in depth. Faced with anything foreign, the Established Order knows only two types of behaviour, which are both mutilating: either to acknowledge it as a Punch and Judy show, or to defuse it as a pure reflection of the West. In any case, the main thing is to deprive it of its history. We see therefore that the 'beautiful pictures' of *The Lost Continent* cannot be innocent: it cannot be innocent to *lose* the continent which found itself again at Bandoeng.

Plastic

Despite having names of Greek shepherds (Polystyrene, Polyvinyl, Polyethylene), plastic, the products of which have just been gathered in an exhibition, is in essence the stuff of alchemy. At the entrance of the stand, the public waits in a long queue in order to witness the accomplishment of the magical operation par excellence: the transmutation of matter. An ideally-shaped machine, tubulated and oblong (a shape well suited to suggest the secret of an itinerary) effortlessly draws, out of a heap of greenish crystals, shiny and fluted dressing-room tidies. At one end, raw, telluric matter, at the other, the finished, human object; and between these two extremes, nothing; nothing but a transit, hardly watched over by an attendant in a cloth cap, half-god, half-robot.

So, more than a substance, plastic is the very idea of its infinite transformation; as its everyday name indicates, it is ubiquity made visible. And it is this, in fact, which makes it a miraculous substance: a miracle is always a sudden transformation of nature. Plastic remains impregnated throughout with this wonder: it is less a thing than the trace of a movement.

And as the movement here is almost infinite, transforming the original crystals into a multitude of more and more startling objects, plastic is, all told, a spectacle to be deciphered: the very spectacle of its end-products. At the sight of each terminal form (suitcase, brush, car-body, toy, fabric, tube, basin or paper), the mind does not cease from considering the original matter as an enigma. This is because the quick-change artistry of plastic is absolute: it can become buckets as well as jewels. Hence a perpetual amazement, the reverie of man at the sight of the proliferating forms of matter, and the connections he detects between the singular of the origin and the plural of the effects. And this amazement is a pleasurable one, since the scope of the transformations gives man the measure of his power, and since the very itinerary of plastic gives him the euphoria of a prestigious free-wheeling through Nature.

But the price to be paid for this success is that plastic, sublimated as movement, hardly exists as substance. Its reality is a negative one: neither hard nor deep, it must be content with a 'substantial' attribute which is neutral in spite of its utilitarian advantages: *resistance*, a state which merely means an absence of yielding. In the hierarchy of the major poetic substances, it figures as a disgraced material, lost between the effusiveness of rubber and the flat hardness of metal; it embodies none of the genuine produce of the mineral world: foam, fibres, strata. It is a 'shaped' substance: whatever its final state, plastic keeps a flocculent appearance, something opaque, creamy and curdled, something powerless ever to achieve the triumphant smoothness of Nature. But what best reveals it for what it is is the sound it gives, at once hollow and flat; its noise is its undoing, as are its colours, for it seems capable of retaining only the most chemical-looking ones. Of yellow, red and green, it keeps only the aggressive quality, and uses them as mere names, being able to display only concepts of colours.

The fashion for plastic highlights an evolution in the myth of 'imitation' materials. It is well known that their use is historically bourgeois in origin (the first vestimentary postiches date back to the rise of capitalism). But until now imitation materials have always indicated pretension, they belonged to the world of appearances, not to that of actual use; they aimed at reproducing cheaply the rarest substances, diamonds, silk, feathers, furs, silver, all the luxurious brilliance of the world. Plastic has climbed down, it is a household material. It is the first magical substance which consents to be prosaic. But it is precisely because this prosaic character is a triumphant reason for its existence: for the first time, artifice aims at something common, not rare. And as an immediate consequence, the age-old function of nature is modified: it is no longer the Idea, the pure Substance to be regained or imitated: an artificial Matter, more bountiful than all the natural deposits, is about to replace her, and to determine the very invention of forms. A luxurious object is still of this earth, it still recalls, albeit in a precious mode, its mineral or animal origin, the natural theme of which it is but one actualization. Plastic is wholly swallowed up in the fact of being used: ultimately, objects will be invented for the sole pleasure of using them. The hierarchy of substances is abolished: a single one replaces them all: the whole world *can* be plasticized, and even life itself since, we are told, they are beginning to make plastic aortas.

The Great Family of Man

A big exhibition of photographs has been held in Paris, the aim of which was to show the universality of human actions in the daily life of all the countries of the world: birth, death, work, knowledge, play, always impose the same types of behaviour; there is a family of Man.

The Family of Man, such at any rate was the original title of the exhibition which came here from the United States. The French have translated it as: *The Great Family of Man*. So what could originally pass for a phrase belonging to zoology, keeping only the similarity in behaviour, the unity of a species, is here amply moralized and sentimentalized. We are at the outset directed to this ambiguous myth of the human 'community', which serves as an alibi to a large part of our humanism.

This myth functions in two stages: first the difference between human morphologies is asserted, exoticism is insistently stressed, the infinite variations of the species, the diversity in skins, skulls and customs are made manifest, the image of Babel is complacently projected over that of the world. Then, from this pluralism, a type of unity is magically produced: man is born, works, laughs and dies everywhere in the same way; and if there still remains in these actions some ethnic peculiarity, at least one hints that there is underlying each one an identical 'nature', that their diversity is only formal and does not belie the existence of a common mould. Of course this means postulating a human essence, and here is God re-introduced into our Exhibition: the diversity of men proclaims his power, his richness; the unity of their gestures demonstrates his will. This is what the introductory leaflet confides to us when it states, by the pen of M. André Chamson, that '*this look over the human condition must somewhat resemble the benevolent gaze of God on our absurd and sublime ant-hill*'. The pietistic intention is underlined by the quotations which accompany each chapter of the Exhibition: these quotations often are 'primitive' proverbs or verses from the Old Testament. They all define an eternal wisdom, a class of assertions which escape History: '*The Earth is a Mother who never dies, Eat bread and salt and speak the truth*, etc.' This is the reign of gnomic truths, the meeting of all the ages of humanity at the most neutral point of their nature, the point where the obviousness of the truism has no longer any value except in the realm of a purely 'poetic' language. Everything here, the content and appeal of the pictures, the discourse which justifies them, aims to suppress the determining weight of History: we are held back at the surface of an identity, prevented precisely by sentimentality from penetrating into this ulterior zone of human behaviour where historical alienation introduces some 'differences' which we shall here quite simply call 'injustices'.

This myth of the human 'condition' rests on a very old mystification, which always consists in placing Nature at the bottom of History. Any classic humanism postulates that in scratching the history of men a little, the relativity of their institutions or the superficial diversity of their skins (but why not ask the parents of Emmet Till, the young Negro assassinated by the Whites what *they* think of *The Great Family of Man*?), one very quickly reaches the solid rock of a universal human nature. Progressive humanism, on the contrary, must always remember to reverse the terms of this very old imposture, constantly to scour nature, its 'laws' and its 'limits' in order to discover History there, and at last to establish Nature itself as historical.

Examples? Here they are: those of our Exhibition. Birth, death? Yes, these are facts of nature, universal facts. But if one removes History from them, there is nothing more to be said about them; any comment about them becomes purely tautological. The failure of photography seems to me to be flagrant in this connection: to reproduce death or birth tells us, literally, nothing. For these natural facts to gain access to a true language, they must be inserted into a category of knowledge which means postulating that one can transform them, and precisely subject their naturalness to our human criticism. For however universal, they are the signs of an historical writing. True, children are *always* born:

but in the whole mass of the human problem, what does the 'essence' of this process matter to us, compared to its modes which, as for them, are perfectly historical? Whether or not the child is born with ease or difficulty, whether or not his birth causes suffering to his mother, whether or not he is threatened by a high mortality rate, whether or not such and such a type of future is open to him: this is what your Exhibitions should be telling people, instead of an eternal lyricism of birth. The same goes for death: must we really celebrate its essence once more, and thus risk forgetting that there is still so much we can do to fight it? It is this very young, far too young power that we must exalt, and not the sterile identity of 'natural' death.

And what can be said about work, which the Exhibition places among great universal facts, putting it on the same plane as birth and death, as if it was quite evident that it belongs to the same order of fate? That work is an age-old fact does not in the least prevent it from remaining a perfectly historical fact. Firstly, and evidently, because of its modes, its motivations, its ends and its benefits, which matter to such an extent that it will never be fair to confuse in a purely gestural identity the colonial and the Western worker (let us also ask the North African workers of the Goutte d'Or district in Paris what they think of *The Great Family of Man*). Secondly, because of the very differences in its inevitability: we know very well that work is 'natural' just as long as it is 'profitable', and that in modifying the inevitability of the profit, we shall perhaps one day modify the inevitability of labour. It is this entirely historified work which we should be told about, instead of an eternal aesthetics of laborious gestures.

So that I rather fear that the final justification of all this Adamism is to give to the immobility of the world the alibi of a 'wisdom' and a 'lyricism' which only make the gestures of man look eternal the better to defuse them.

The Lady of the Camellias

They still perform, in some part of the world or other, *The Lady of the Camellias* (it had in fact another run in Paris some time ago). This success must alert us to a mythology of Love which probably still exists, for the alienation of Marguerite Gautier in relation to the class of her masters is not fundamentally different from that of today's petit-bourgeois women in a world which is just as stratified.

Yet in fact, the central myth in *The Lady of the Camellias* is not Love, it is Recognition. Marguerite loves in order to achieve recognition, and this is why her passion (in the etymological, not the libidinal sense) has its source entirely in other people. Armand, on the other hand (who is the son of a District Collector of Taxes), gives an example of classical love: bourgeois, descended from essentialist culture, and one which will live on in Proust's analyses. This is a segregative love, that of the owner who carries off his prey; an internalized love, which acknowledges the existence of the world only intermittently and always with a feeling of frustration, as if the world were never anything but the threat of some theft (jealousy, quarrels, misunderstandings, worry, coolness, irritation, etc.). Marguerite's Love is the perfect opposite of this. She was first touched to feel herself *recognized* by Armand, and passion, to her, was thereafter nothing but the permanent demand for this recognition; this is why the sacrifice which she grants M. Duval in renouncing Armand is by no means moral (in spite of the phraseology used), it is existential; it is only the logical consequence of the postulate of recognition, a superlative means (much better than love) of winning recognition from the world of the masters. And if Marguerite hides her sacrifice and gives it the mask of cynicism, this can only be at the moment when the argument really becomes Literature: the grateful and recognizing gaze of the bourgeois class is here delegated to the reader who in his turn *recognizes* Marguerite through the very mistake of her lover.

All this is to say that the misunderstandings which make the plot progress are not here of a psychological nature (even if the language in which they are expressed is abusively so): Armand and Marguerite do not belong socially to the same world and there can be no question between them of tragedy in the manner of Racine or subtle flirting in the manner of Marivaux. The conflict is exterior to them: we do not deal here with one passion divided against itself but with two passions of different natures, because they come from different situations in society. Armand's passion, which is bourgeois in type, and appropriative, is by definition a murder of the other; and that of Marguerite can only crown her effort to achieve recognition by a sacrifice which will in its turn constitute an indirect murder of Armand's passion. A simple social disparity, taken up and amplified by the opposition of two ideologies of love, cannot but produce here a hopeless entanglement, a hopelessness of which Marguerite's death (however cloying it is on the stage) is, so to speak, the algebraic symbol.

The difference between the two types of love stems of course from the difference of awareness in the two partners: Armand lives in the essence of eternal love, Marguerite lives in the awareness of her alienation, she lives only through it: she knows herself to be, and in a sense *wills* herself to be a courtesan. And the behaviour she adopts in order to adjust consists entirely in behaviour meant to secure recognition: now she endorses her own legend exaggeratedly, and plunges into the whirlwind of the typical courtesan's life (like those homosexuals whose way of accepting their condition is to make it obvious), sometimes she makes one guess at a power to transcend her rank which aims to achieve recognition less for a 'natural' virtue than for a devotion suited to her station, as if her sacrifice had the function, not of making manifest the murder of the courtesan she is, but on the contrary of flaunting a superlative courtesan, enhanced, without losing anything of her nature, with a bourgeois feeling of a high order.

Thus we begin to see better the mythological content of this love, which is the archetype of petit-bourgeois sentimentality. It is a very particular state of myth, defined by a semi-awareness, or to be more precise, a parasitic awareness. Marguerite *is aware* of her alienation, that is to say she sees reality as an alienation. But she follows up this awareness by a purely servile behaviour: either she plays the part which the masters expect from her, or she tries to reach a *value* which is in fact a part of this same world of the masters. In either case, Marguerite is never anything more than an alienated awareness: she sees that she suffers, but imagines no remedy which is not parasitic to her own suffering; she knows herself to be an object but cannot think of any destination for herself other than that of ornament in the museum of the masters. In spite of the grotesqueness of the plot, such a character does not lack a certain dramatic richness: true, it is neither tragic (the fate which weighs on Marguerite is social, not metaphysical), nor comic (Marguerite's behaviour stems from her condition, not from her essence), nor as yet, of course, revolutionary (Marguerite brings no criticism to bear on her alienation). But at bottom she would need very little to achieve the status of the Brechtian character, which is an alienated object but a source of criticism. What puts this out of her reach — irremediably — is her positive side: Marguerite Gautier, 'touching' because of her tuberculosis and her lofty speech, spreads to the whole of her public the contagion of her blindness: patently stupid, she would have opened their petit-bourgeois eyes. Magniloquent and noble, in one word 'serious', she only sends them to sleep.

MYTH TODAY

Myth Today

What is a myth, today? I shall give at the outset a first, very simple answer, which is perfectly consistent with etymology: *myth is a type of speech*.[1]

Myth is a type of speech

Of course, it is not *any* type: language needs special conditions in order to become myth: we shall see them in a minute. But what must be firmly established at the start is that myth is a system of communication, that it is a message. This allows one to perceive that myth cannot possibly be an object, a concept, or an idea; it is a mode of signification, a form. Later, we shall have to assign to this form historical limits, conditions of use, and reintroduce society into it: we must nevertheless first describe it as a form.

It can be seen that to purport to discriminate among mythical objects according to their substance would be entirely illusory: since myth is a type of speech, everything can be a myth provided it is conveyed by a discourse. Myth is not defined by the object of its message, but by the way in which it utters this message: there are formal limits to myth, there are no 'substantial' ones. Everything, then, can be a myth? Yes, I believe this, for the universe is infinitely fertile in suggestions. Every object in the world can pass from a closed, silent existence to an oral state, open to appropriation by society, for there is no law, whether natural or not, which forbids talking about things. A tree is a tree. Yes, of course. But a tree as expressed by Minou Drouet is no longer quite a tree, it is a tree which is decorated, adapted to a certain type of consumption, laden with literary self-indulgence, revolt, images, in short with a type of social *usage* which is added to pure matter.

[1] Innumerable other meanings of the word 'myth' can be cited against this. But I have tried to define things, not words.

Naturally, everything is not expressed at the same time: some objects become the prey of mythical speech for a while, then they disappear, others take their place and attain the status of myth. Are there objects which are *inevitably* a source of suggestiveness, as Baudelaire suggested about Woman? Certainly not: one can conceive of very ancient myths, but there are no eternal ones; for it is human history which converts reality into speech, and it alone rules the life and the death of mythical language. Ancient or not, mythology can only have an historical foundation, for myth is a type of speech chosen by history: it cannot possibly evolve from the 'nature' of things.

Speech of this kind is a message. It is therefore by no means confined to oral speech. It can consist of modes of writing or of representations; not only written discourse, but also photography, cinema, reporting, sport, shows, publicity, all these can serve as a support to mythical speech. Myth can be defined neither by its object nor by its material, for any material can arbitrarily be endowed with meaning: the arrow which is brought in order to signify a challenge is also a kind of speech. True, as far as perception is concerned, writing and pictures, for instance, do not call upon the same type of consciousness; and even with pictures, one can use many kinds of reading: a diagram lends itself to signification more than a drawing, a copy more than an original, and a caricature more than a portrait. But this is the point: we are no longer dealing here with a theoretical mode of representation: we are dealing with *this* particular image, which is given for *this* particular signification. Mythical speech is made of a material which has *already* been worked on so as to make it suitable for communication: it is because all the materials of myth (whether pictorial or written) presuppose a signifying consciousness, that one can reason about them while discounting their substance. This substance is not unimportant: pictures, to be sure, are more imperative than writing, they impose meaning at one stroke, without analysing or diluting it. But this is no longer a constitutive difference. Pictures become a kind of writing as soon as they are meaningful: like writing, they call for a *lexis*.

We shall therefore take *language*, *discourse*, *speech*, etc., to mean any significant unit or synthesis, whether verbal or visual: a photograph will be a kind of speech for us in the same way as a newspaper article; even objects will become speech, if they mean something. This generic way of conceiving language is in fact justified by the very history of writing: long before the invention of our alphabet, objects like the Inca *quipu*, or drawings, as in pictographs, have been accepted as speech. This does not mean that one must treat mythical speech like language; myth in fact belongs to the province of a general science, coextensive with linguistics, which is *semiology*.

Myth as a semiological system

For mythology, since it is the study of a type of speech, is but one fragment of this vast science of signs which Saussure postulated some forty years ago under the name of *semiology*. Semiology has not yet come into being. But since Saussure himself, and sometimes independently of him, a whole section of contemporary research has constantly been referred to the problem of meaning: psycho-analysis, structuralism, eidetic psychology, some new types of literary criticism of which Bachelard has given the first examples, are no longer concerned with facts except inasmuch as they are endowed with significance. Now to postulate a signification is to have recourse to semiology. I do not mean that semiology could account for all these aspects of research equally well: they have different contents. But they have a common status: they are all sciences dealing with values. They are not content with meeting the facts: they define and explore them as tokens for something else.

Semiology is a science of forms, since it studies significations apart from their content. I should like to say one word about the necessity and the limits of such a formal science. The necessity is that which applies in the case of any exact language. Zhdanov made fun of Alexandrov the philosopher, who spoke of '*the spherical structure of our planet.*' '*It was thought until now*', Zhdanov said, '*that form alone could be spherical.*' Zhdanov was right: one cannot speak about structures in terms of forms, and vice versa. It may well be that on the plane of 'life', there is but a totality where structures and forms cannot be separated. But science has no use for the ineffable: it must speak about 'life' if it wants to transform it. Against a certain quixotism of synthesis, quite platonic incidentally, all criticism must consent to the *ascesis*, to the artifice of analysis; and in analysis, it must match method and language. Less terrorized by the spectre of 'formalism', historical criticism might have been less sterile; it would have understood that the specific study of forms does not in any way contradict the necessary principles of totality and History. On the contrary: the more a system is specifically defined in its forms, the more amenable it is to historical criticism. To parody a well-known saying, I shall say that a little formalism turns one away from History, but that a lot brings one back to it. Is there a better example of total criticism than the description of saintliness, at once formal and historical, semiological and ideological, in Sartre's *Saint-Genet*? The danger, on the contrary, is to consider forms as ambiguous objects, half-form and half-substance, to endow form with a substance of form, as was done, for instance, by Zhdanovian realism. Semiology, once its limits are settled, is not a metaphysical trap: it is a science among others, necessary but not sufficient. The important thing is to see that the unity of an explanation cannot be based on the amputation of one or other of its approaches, but, as Engels said, on the dialectical co-ordination of the particular sciences it makes use of. This is the case with mythology: it is a part both of semiology inasmuch as it is a formal science, and of ideology inasmuch as it is an historical science: it studies ideas-in-form.[2]

Let me therefore restate that any semiology postulates a relation between two terms, a signifier and a signified. This relation concerns objects which belong to different categories, and this is why it is not one of equality but one of equivalence. We

[2] The development of publicity, of a national press, of radio, of illustrated news, not to speak of the survival of a myriad rites of communication which rule social appearances makes the development of a semiological science more urgent than ever. In a single day, how many really non-signifying fields do we cross? Very few, sometimes none. Here I am, before the sea; it is true that it bears no message. But on the beach, what material for semiology! Flags, slogans, signals, sign-boards, clothes, suntan even, which are so many messages to me.

must here be on our guard for despite common parlance which simply says that the signifier *expresses* the signified, we are dealing, in any semiological system, not with two, but with three different terms. For what we grasp is not at all one term after the other, but the correlation which unites them: there are, therefore, the signifier, the signified and the sign, which is the associative total of the first two terms. Take a bunch of roses: I use it to *signify* my passion. Do we have here, then, only a signifier and a signified, the roses and my passion? Not even that: to put it accurately, there are here only 'passionified' roses. But on the plane of analysis, we do have three terms; for these roses weighted with passion perfectly and correctly allow themselves to be decomposed into roses and passion: the former and the latter existed before uniting and forming this third object, which is the sign. It is as true to say that on the plane of experience I cannot dissociate the roses from the message they carry, as to say that on the plane of analysis I cannot confuse the roses as signifier and the roses as sign: the signifier is empty, the sign is full, it is a meaning. Or take a black pebble: I can make it signify in several ways, it is a mere signifier; but if I weigh it with a definite signified (a death sentence, for instance, in an anonymous vote), it will become a sign. Naturally, there are between the signifier, the signified and the sign, functional implications (such as that of the part to the whole) which are so close that to analyse them may seem futile; but we shall see in a moment that this distinction has a capital importance for the study of myth as semiological schema.

Naturally these three terms are purely formal, and different contents can be given to them. Here are a few examples: for Saussure, who worked on a particular but methodologically exemplary semiological system—the language or *langue*—the signified is the concept, the signifier is the acoustic image (which is mental) and the relation between concept and image is the sign (the word, for instance), which is a concrete entity.[3] For Freud, as is well known, the human psyche is a stratification of tokens or

[3] The notion of *word* is one of the most controversial in linguistics. I keep it here for the sake of simplicity.

representatives. One term (I refrain from giving it any precedence) is constituted by the manifest meaning of behaviour, another, by its latent or real meaning (it is, for instance, the substratum of the dream); as for the third term, it is here also a correlation of the first two: it is the dream itself in its totality, the parapraxis (a mistake in speech or behaviour) or the neurosis, conceived as compromises, as economies effected thanks to the joining of a form (the first term) and an intentional function (the second term). We can see here how necessary it is to distinguish the sign from the signifier: a dream, to Freud, is no more its manifest datum than its latent content: it is the functional union of these two terms. In Sartrean criticism, finally (I shall keep to these three well-known examples), the signified is constituted by the original crisis in the subject (the separation from his mother for Baudelaire, the naming of the theft for Genet); Literature as discourse forms the signifier; and the relation between crisis and discourse defines the work, which is a signification. Of course, this tri-dimensional pattern, however constant in its form, is actualized in different ways: one cannot therefore say too often that semiology can have its unity only at the level of forms, not contents; its field is limited, it knows only one operation: reading, or deciphering.

In myth, we find again the tri-dimensional pattern which I have just described: the signifier, the signified and the sign. But myth is a peculiar system, in that it is constructed from a semiological chain which existed before it: it *is a second-order semiological system*. That which is a sign (namely the associative total of a concept and an image) in the first system, becomes a mere signifier in the second. We must here recall that the materials of mythical speech (the language itself, photography, painting, posters, rituals, objects, etc.), however different at the start, are reduced to a pure signifying function as soon as they are caught by myth. Myth sees in them only the same raw material; their unity is that they all come down to the status of a mere language. Whether it deals with alphabetical or pictorial writing, myth wants to see in them only a sum of signs, a global sign, the final term of a first semiological chain. And it is precisely this final term which will become the first term of the greater system which it builds and of which it is only a part. Everything happens as if myth shifted the formal system of the first significations sideways. As this lateral shift is essential for the analysis of myth, I shall represent it in the following way, it being understood, of course, that the spatialization of the pattern is here only a metaphor:

It can be seen that in myth there are two semiological systems, one of which is staggered in relation to the other: a linguistic system, the language (or the modes of representation which are assimilated to it), which I shall call the *language-object*, because it is the language which myth gets hold of in order to build its own system; and myth itself, which I shall call *metalanguage*, because it is a second language, *in which* one speaks about the first. When he reflects on a metalanguage, the semiologist no longer needs to ask himself questions about the composition of the language-object, he no longer has to take into account the details of the linguistic schema; he will only need to know its total term, or global sign, and only inasmuch as this term lends itself to myth. This is why the semiologist is entitled to treat in the same way writing and pictures: what he retains from them is the fact that they are both *signs*, that they both reach the threshold of myth endowed with the same signifying function, that they constitute, one just as much as the other, a language-object.

It is now time to give one or two examples of mythical speech. I shall borrow the first from an observation by Valéry.[4] I am a pupil in the second form in a French *lycée*. I open my Latin grammar, and I read a sentence, borrowed from Aesop or Phaedrus: *quia ego nominor leo*. I stop and think. There is something ambiguous about this statement: on the one hand, the

[4] *Tel Quel*, II, p. 191.

words in it do have a simple meaning: *because my name is lion*. And on the other hand, the sentence is evidently there in order to signify something else to me. Inasmuch as it is addressed to me, a pupil in the second form, it tells me clearly: I am a grammatical example meant to illustrate the rule about the agreement of the predicate. I am even forced to realize that the sentence in no way *signifies* its meaning to me, that it tries very little to tell me something about the lion and what sort of name he has; its true and fundamental signification is to impose itself on me as the presence of a certain agreement of the predicate. I conclude that I am faced with a particular, greater, semiological system, since it is co-extensive with the language: there is, indeed, a signifier, but this signifier is itself formed by a sum of signs, it is in itself a first semiological system (*my name is lion*). Thereafter, the formal pattern is correctly unfolded: there is a signified (*I am a grammatical example*) and there is a global signification, which is none other than the correlation of the signifier and the signified; for neither the naming of the lion nor the grammatical example are given separately.

And here is now another example: I am at the barber's, and a copy of *Paris-Match* is offered to me. On the cover, a young Negro in a French uniform is saluting, with his eyes uplifted, probably fixed on a fold of the tricolour. All this is the *meaning* of the picture. But, whether naively or not, I see very well what it signifies to me: that France is a great Empire, that all her sons, without any colour discrimination, faithfully serve under her flag, and that there is no better answer to the detractors of an alleged colonialism than the zeal shown by this Negro in serving his so-called oppressors. I am therefore again faced with a greater semiological system: there is a signifier, itself already formed with a previous system (*a black soldier is giving the French salute*); there is a signified (it is here a purposeful mixture of Frenchness and militariness); finally, there is a presence of the signified through the signifier.

Before tackling the analysis of each term of the mythical system, one must agree on terminology. We now know that the signifier can be looked at, in myth, from two points of view: as the final term of the linguistic system, or as the first term of the mythical system. We therefore need two names. On the plane of language, that is, as the final term of the first system, I shall call the signifier: *meaning* (*my name is lion, a Negro is giving the French salute*); on the plane of myth, I shall call it: *form*. In the case of the signified, no ambiguity is possible: we shall retain the name *concept*. The third term is the correlation of the first two: in the linguistic system, it is the *sign*; but it is not possible to use this word again without ambiguity, since in myth (and this is the chief peculiarity of the latter), the signifier is already formed by the *signs* of the language. I shall call the third term of myth the *signification*. This word is here all the better justified since myth has in fact a double function: it points out and it notifies, it makes us understand something and it imposes it on us.

The form and the concept

The signifier of myth presents itself in an ambiguous way: it is at the same time meaning and form, full on one side and empty on the other. As meaning, the signifier already postulates a reading, I grasp it through my eyes, it has a sensory reality (unlike the linguistic signifier, which is purely mental), there is a richness in it: the naming of the lion, the Negro's salute are credible wholes, they have at their disposal a sufficient rationality. As a total of linguistic signs, the meaning of the myth has its own value, it belongs to a history, that of the lion or that of the Negro: in the meaning, a signification is already built, and could very well be self-sufficient if myth did not take hold of it and did not turn it suddenly into an empty, parasitical form. The meaning is *already* complete, it postulates a kind of knowledge, a past, a memory, a comparative order of facts, ideas, decisions.

When it becomes form, the meaning leaves its contingency behind; it empties itself, it becomes impoverished, history evaporates, only the letter remains. There is here a paradoxical permutation in the reading operations, an abnormal regression from meaning to form, from the linguistic sign to the mythical signifier. If one encloses *quia ego nominor leo* in a purely linguistic system, the clause finds again there a fullness, a richness, a history: I am an animal, a lion, I live in a certain country, I have just been hunting, they would have me share my prey with a heifer, a cow and a goat; but being the stronger, I award myself all the shares for various reasons, the last of which is quite simply that *my name is lion*. But as the form of the myth, the clause hardly retains anything of this long story. The meaning contained a whole system of values: a history, a geography, a morality, a zoology, a Literature. The form has put all this richness at a distance: its newly acquired penury calls for a signification to fill it. The story of the lion must recede a great deal in order to make room for the grammatical example, one must put the biography of the Negro in parentheses if one wants to free the picture, and prepare it to receive its signified.

But the essential point in all this is that the form does not suppress the meaning, it only impoverishes it, it puts it at a distance, it holds it at one's disposal. One believes that the meaning is going to die, but it is a death with reprieve; the meaning loses its value, but keeps its life, from which the form of the myth will draw its nourishment. The meaning will be for the form like an instantaneous reserve of history, a tamed richness, which it is possible to call and dismiss in a sort of rapid alternation: the form must constantly be able to be rooted again in the meaning and to get there what nature it needs for its nutriment; above all, it must be able to hide there. It is this constant game of hide-and-seek between the meaning and the form which defines myth. The form of myth is not a symbol: the Negro who salutes is not the symbol of the French Empire: he has too much presence, he appears as a rich, fully experienced, spontaneous, innocent, *indisputable* image. But at the same time this presence is tamed, put at a distance, made almost transparent; it recedes a little, it becomes the accomplice of a concept which comes to it fully armed, French imperiality: once made use of, it becomes artificial.

Let us now look at the signified: this history which drains out of the form will be wholly absorbed by the concept. As for the latter, it is determined, it is at once historical and intentional; it is the motivation which causes the myth to be uttered. Grammatical exemplarity, French imperiality, are the very drives behind the myth. The concept reconstitutes a chain of causes and effects, motives and intentions. Unlike the form, the concept is in no way abstract: it is filled with a situation. Through the concept, it is a whole new history which is implanted in the myth. Into the naming of the lion, first drained of its contingency, the grammatical example will attract my whole existence: Time, which caused me to be born at a certain period when Latin grammar is taught; History, which sets me apart, through a whole mechanism of social segregation, from the children who do not learn Latin; paedagogic tradition, which caused this example to be chosen from Aesop or Phaedrus; my own linguistic habits, which see the agreement of the predicate as a fact worthy of notice and illustration. The same goes for the Negro-giving-the-salute: as form, its meaning is shallow, isolated, impoverished; as the concept of French imperiality, here it is again tied to the totality of the world: to the general History of France, to its colonial adventures, to its present difficulties. Truth to tell, what is invested in the concept is less reality than a certain knowledge of reality; in passing from the meaning to the form, the image loses some knowledge: the better to receive the knowledge in the concept. In actual fact, the knowledge contained in a mythical concept is confused, made of yielding, shapeless associations. One must firmly stress this open character of the concept; it is not at all an abstract, purified essence; it is a formless, unstable, nebulous condensation, whose unity and coherence are above all due to its function.

In this sense, we can say that the fundamental character of the mythical concept is to be *appropriated*: grammatical exemplarity very precisely concerns a given form of pupils, French imperiality must appeal to such and such group of readers and not another. The concept closely corresponds to a function, it is defined as a tendency. This cannot fail to recall the signified in another semiological system, Freudianism. In Freud, the second term of the system is the latent meaning (the content) of the dream, of the parapraxis, of the neurosis. Now Freud does remark that the second-order meaning of behaviour is its real meaning, that which is appropriate to a complete situation, including its deeper level; it is, just like the mythical concept, the very intention of behaviour.

A signified can have several signifiers: this is indeed the case in linguistics and psycho-analysis. It is also the case in the mythical concept: it has at its disposal an unlimited mass of signifiers: I can find a thousand Latin sentences to actualize for me the agreement of the predicate, I can find a thousand images which signify to me French imperiality. This means that *quantitively*, the concept is much poorer than the signifier, it often does nothing but re-present itself. Poverty and richness are in reverse proportion in the form and the concept: to the qualitative poverty of the form, which is the repository of a rarefied meaning, there corresponds the richness of the concept which is open to the whole of History; and to the quantitative abundance of the forms there corresponds a small number of concepts. This repetition of the concept through different forms is precious to the mythologist, it allows him to decipher the myth: it is the insistence of a kind of behaviour which reveals its intention. This confirms that there is no regular ratio between the volume of the signified and that of the signifier. In language, this ratio is proportionate, it hardly exceeds the word, or at least the concrete unit. In myth, on the contrary, the concept can spread over a very large expanse of signifier. For instance, a whole book may be the signifier of a single concept; and conversely, a minute form (a word, a gesture, even incidental, so long as it is noticed) can serve as signifier to a concept filled with a very rich history. Although unusual in language, this disproportion between signifier and signified is not specific to myth: in Freud, for instance, the parapraxis is a signifier whose thinness is out of proportion to the real meaning which it betrays.

As I said, there is no fixity in mythical concepts: they can come into being, alter, disintegrate, disappear completely. And it is precisely because they are historical that history can very easily suppress them. This instability forces the mythologist to use a terminology adapted to it, and about which I should now like to say a word, because it often is a cause for irony: I mean neologism. The concept is a constituting element of myth: if I want to decipher myths, I must somehow be able to name concepts. The dictionary supplies me with a few: Goodness, Kindness, Wholeness, Humaneness, etc. But by definition, since it is the dictionary which gives them to me, these particular concepts are not historical. Now what I need most often is ephemeral concepts, in connection with limited contingencies: neologism is then inevitable. China is one thing, the idea which a French petit-bourgeois could have of it not so long ago is another: for this peculiar mixture of bells, rickshaws and opium-dens, no other word possible but *Sininess*.[5] Unlovely? One should at least get some consolation from the fact that conceptual neologisms are never arbitrary: they are built according to a highly sensible proportional rule.

The signification

In semiology, the third term is nothing but the association of the first two, as we saw. It is the only one which is allowed to be seen in a full and satisfactory way, the only one which is consumed in actual fact. I have called it: the signification. We can see that the signification is the myth itself, just as the Saussurean sign is the word (or more accurately the concrete unit). But before listing the characters of the signification, one must reflect a little on the way in which it is prepared, that is, on the modes of correlation of the mythical concept and the mythical form.

First we must note that in myth, the first two terms are perfectly manifest (unlike what happens in other semiological systems): one of them is not 'hidden' behind the other, they are both given *here* (and not one here and the other there). However paradoxical it may seem, *myth hides nothing*: its function is to distort, not to make disappear. There is no latency of the concept in relation to the form: there is no need of an unconscious in order to explain myth. Of course, one is dealing with two different types of manifestation: form has a literal, immediate presence; moreover, it is extended. This stems—this cannot be repeated too often—from the nature of the mythical signifier,

[5] Or perhaps *Sinity*? Just as if Latin/latinity = Basque/x, x = Basquity.

which is already linguistic: since it is constituted by a meaning which is already outlined, it can appear only through a given substance (whereas in language, the signifier remains mental). In the case of oral myth, this extension is linear (*for my name is lion*); in that of visual myth, it is multi-dimensional (in the centre, the Negro's uniform, at the top, the blackness of his face, on the left, the military salute, etc.). The elements of the form therefore are related as to place and proximity: the mode of presence of the form is spatial. The concept, on the contrary, appears in global fashion, it is a kind of nebula, the condensation, more or less hazy, of a certain knowledge. Its elements are linked by associative relations: it is supported not by an extension but by a depth (although this metaphor is perhaps still too spatial): its mode of presence is memorial.

The relation which unites the concept of the myth to its meaning is essentially a relation of *deformation*. We find here again a certain formal analogy with a complex semiological system such as that of the various types of psycho-analysis. Just as for Freud the manifest meaning of behaviour is distorted by its latent meaning, in myth the meaning is distorted by the concept. Of course, this distortion is possible only because the form of the myth is already constituted by a linguistic meaning. In a simple system like the language, the signified cannot distort anything at all because the signifier, being empty, arbitrary, offers no resistance to it. But here, everything is different: the signifier has, so to speak, two aspects: one full, which is the meaning (the history of the lion, of the Negro soldier), one empty, which is the form (*for my name is lion*; *Negro-French-soldier-saluting-the-tricolour*). What the concept distorts is of course what is full, the meaning: the lion and the Negro are deprived of their history, changed into gestures. What Latin exemplarity distorts is the naming of the lion, in all its contingency; and what French imperiality obscures is also a primary language, a factual discourse which was telling me about the salute of a Negro in uniform. But this distortion is not an obliteration: the lion and the Negro remain here, the concept needs them; they are half-amputated, they are deprived of memory, not of existence: they are at once stubborn, silently rooted there, and garrulous, a speech wholly at the service of the concept. The concept, literally, deforms, but does not abolish the meaning; a word can perfectly render this contradiction: it alienates it.

What must always be remembered is that myth is a double system; there occurs in it a sort of ubiquity: its point of departure is constituted by the arrival of a meaning. To keep a spatial metaphor, the approximative character of which I have already stressed, I shall say that the signification of the myth is constituted by a sort of constantly moving turnstile which presents alternately the meaning of the signifier and its form, a language-object and a metalanguage, a purely signifying and a purely imagining consciousness. This alternation is, so to speak, gathered up in the concept, which uses it like an ambiguous signifier, at once intellective and imaginary, arbitrary and natural.

I do not wish to prejudge the moral implications of such a mechanism, but I shall not exceed the limits of an objective analysis if I point out that the ubiquity of the signifier in myth exactly reproduces the physique of the *alibi* (which is, as one realizes, a spatial term): in the alibi too, there is a place which is full and one which is empty, linked by a relation of negative identity ('I am not where you think I am; I am where you think I am not'). But the ordinary alibi (for the police, for instance) has an end; reality stops the turnstile revolving at a certain point. Myth is a *value*, truth is no guarantee for it; nothing prevents it from being a perpetual alibi: it is enough that its signifier has two sides for it always to have an 'elsewhere' at its disposal. The meaning is always there to *present* the form; the form is always there to *outdistance* the meaning. And there never is any contradiction, conflict, or split between the meaning and the form: they are never at the same place. In the same way, if I am in a car and I look at the scenery through the window, I can at will focus on the scenery or on the window-pane. At one moment I grasp the presence of the glass and the distance of the landscape; at another, on the contrary, the transparence of the glass and the depth of the landscape; but the result of this alternation is constant: the glass is at once present and empty to me, and the landscape unreal and full. The same thing occurs in the mythical signifier: its form is empty but present, its meaning absent but full. To wonder at this contradiction I must voluntarily interrupt this turnstile of form and meaning, I must focus on each separately, and apply to myth a static method of deciphering, in short, I must go against its own dynamics: to sum up, I must pass from the state of reader to that of mythologist.

And it is again this duplicity of the signifier which determines the characters of the signification. We now know that myth is a type of speech defined by its intention (*I am a grammatical example*) much more than by its literal sense (*my name is lion*); and that in spite of this, its intention is somehow frozen, purified, eternalized, *made absent* by this literal sense (*The French Empire? It's just a fact: look at this good Negro who salutes like one of our own boys*). This constituent ambiguity of mythical speech has two consequences for the signification, which henceforth appears both like a notification and like a statement of fact.

Myth has an imperative, buttonholing character: stemming from an historical concept, directly springing from contingency (a Latin class, a threatened Empire), it is *I* whom it has come to seek. It is turned towards me, I am subjected to its intentional force, it summons me to receive its expansive ambiguity. If, for instance, I take a walk in Spain, in the Basque country,[6] I may well notice in the houses an architectural unity, a common style, which leads me to acknowledge the Basque house as a definite ethnic product. However, I do not feel personally concerned, nor, so to speak, attacked by this unitary style: I see only too well that it was here before me, without me. It is a complex product which has its determinations at the level of a very wide history: it does not call out to me, it does not provoke me into naming it, except if I think of inserting it into a vast picture of rural habitat. But if I am in the Paris region and I catch a glimpse, at the end of the rue Gambetta or the rue Jean-Jaurès, of a natty white chalet with red tiles, dark brown half-timbering, an asymmetrical roof and a wattle-and-daub front, I feel as if I were personally

---

[6] I say 'in Spain' because, in France, petit-bourgeois advancement has caused a whole 'mythical' architecture of the Basque chalet to flourish.

receiving an imperious injunction to name this object a Basque chalet: or even better, to see it as the very essence of *basquity*. This is because the concept appears to me in all its appropriative nature: it comes and seeks me out in order to oblige me to acknowledge the body of intentions which have motivated it and arranged it there as the signal of an individual history, as a confidence and a complicity: it is a real call, which the owners of the chalet send out to me. And this call, in order to be more imperious, has agreed to all manner of impoverishments: all that justified the Basque house on the plane of technology — the barn, the outside stairs, the dove-cote, etc. — has been dropped; there remains only a brief order, not to be disputed. And the adhomination is so frank that I feel this chalet has just been created on the spot, *for me*, like a magical object springing up in my present life without any trace of the history which has caused it.

For this interpellant speech is at the same time a frozen speech: at the moment of reaching me, it suspends itself, turns away and assumes the look of a generality: it stiffens, it makes itself look neutral and innocent. The appropriation of the concept is suddenly driven away once more by the literalness of the meaning. This is a kind of *arrest*, in both the physical and the legal sense of the term: French imperiality condemns the saluting Negro to be nothing more than an instrumental signifier, the Negro suddenly hails me in the name of French imperiality; but at the same moment the Negro's salute thickens, becomes vitrified, freezes into an eternal reference meant to *establish* French imperiality. On the surface of language something has stopped moving: the use of the signification is here, hiding behind the fact, and conferring on it a notifying look; but at the same time, the fact paralyses the intention, gives it something like a malaise producing immobility: in order to make it innocent, it freezes it. This is because myth is speech *stolen and restored*. Only, speech which is restored is no longer quite that which was stolen: when it was brought back, it was not put exactly in its place. It is this brief act of larceny, this moment taken for a surreptitious faking, which gives mythical speech its benumbed look.

One last element of the signification remains to be examined:

its motivation. We know that in a language, the sign is arbitrary: nothing compels the acoustic image *tree* 'naturally' to mean the concept *tree*: the sign, here, is unmotivated. Yet this arbitrariness has limits, which come from the associative relations of the word: the language can produce a whole fragment of the sign by analogy with other signs (for instance one says *aimable* in French, and not *amable*, by analogy with *aime*). The mythical signification, on the other hand, is never arbitrary; it is always in part motivated, and unavoidably contains some analogy. For Latin exemplarity to meet the naming of the lion, there must be an analogy, which is the agreement of the predicate; for French imperiality to get hold of the saluting Negro, there must be identity between the Negro's salute and that of the French soldier. Motivation is necessary to the very duplicity of myth: myth plays on the analogy between meaning and form, there is no myth without motivated form.[7] In order to grasp the power of motivation in myth, it is enough to reflect for a moment on an extreme case. I have here before me a collection of objects so lacking in order that I can find no *meaning* in it; it would seem that here, deprived of any previous meaning, the form could not root its analogy in anything, and that myth is impossible. But what the form can always give one to read is disorder itself: it can give a signification to the absurd, make the absurd itself a myth. This is what happens when commonsense mythifies surrealism, for instance. Even the absence of motivation does not embarrass myth; for this absence will itself be sufficiently objectified to become legible: and finally, the absence of motivation will become a second-order motivation, and myth will be re-established.

Motivation is unavoidable. It is none the less very fragmentary.

[7] From the point of view of ethics, what is disturbing in myth is precisely that its form is motivated. For if there is a 'health' of language, it is the arbitrariness of the sign which is its grounding. What is sickening in myth is its resort to a false nature, its superabundance of significant forms, as in these objects which decorate their usefulness with a natural appearance. The will to weigh the signification with the full guarantee of nature causes a kind of nausea: myth is too rich, and what is in excess is precisely its motivation. This nausea is like the one I feel before the arts which refuse to choose between *physis* and *anti-physis*, using the first as an ideal and the second as an economy. Ethically, there is a kind of baseness in hedging one's bets.

To start with, it is not 'natural': it is history which supplies its analogies to the form. Then, the analogy between the meaning and the concept is never anything but partial: the form drops many analogous features and keeps only a few: it keeps the sloping roof, the visible beams in the Basque chalet, it abandons the stairs, the barn, the weathered look, etc. One must even go further: a *complete* image would exclude myth, or at least would compel it to seize only its very completeness. This is just what happens in the case of bad painting, which is wholly based on the myth of what is 'filled out' and 'finished' (it is the opposite and symmetrical case of the myth of the absurd: here, the form mythifies an 'absence', there, a surplus). But in general myth prefers to work with poor, incomplete images, where the meaning is already relieved of its fat, and ready for a signification, such as caricatures, pastiches, symbols, etc. Finally, the motivation is chosen among other possible ones: I can very well give to French imperiality many other signifiers beside a Negro's salute: a French general pins a decoration on a one-armed Senegalese, a nun hands a cup of tea to a bed-ridden Arab, a white school-master teaches attentive piccaninnies: the press undertakes every day to demonstrate that the store of mythical signifiers is inexhaustible.

The nature of the mythical signification can in fact be well conveyed by one particular simile: it is neither more nor less arbitrary than an ideograph. Myth is a pure ideographic system, where the forms are still motivated by the concept which they represent while not yet, by a long way, covering the sum of its possibilities for representation. And just as, historically, ideographs have gradually left the concept and have become associated with the sound, thus growing less and less motivated, the worn out state of a myth can be recognized by the arbitrariness of its signification: the whole of Molière is seen in a doctor's ruff.

Reading and deciphering myth

How is a myth received? We must here once more come back

to the duplicity of its signifier, which is at once meaning and form. I can produce three different types of reading by focusing on the one, or the other, or both at the same time.[8]

1. If I focus on an empty signifier, I let the concept fill the form of the myth without ambiguity, and I find myself before a simple system, where the signification becomes literal again: the Negro who salutes is an *example* of French imperiality, he is a *symbol* for it. This type of focusing is, for instance, that of the producer of myths, of the journalist who starts with a concept and seeks a form for it.[9]

2. If I focus on a full signifier, in which I clearly distinguish the meaning and the form, and consequently the distortion which the one imposes on the other, I undo the signification of the myth, and I receive the latter as an imposture: the saluting Negro becomes the *alibi* of French imperiality. This type of focusing is that of the mythologist: he deciphers the myth, he understands a distortion.

3. Finally, if I focus on the mythical signifier as on an inextricable whole made of meaning and form, I receive an ambiguous signification: I respond to the constituting mechanism of myth, to its own dynamics, I become a reader of myths. The saluting Negro is no longer an example or a symbol, still less an alibi: he is the very *presence* of French imperiality.

The first two types of focusing are static, analytical; they destroy the myth, either by making its intention obvious, or by unmasking it: the former is cynical, the latter demystifying. The third type of focusing is dynamic, it consumes the myth according to the very ends built into its structure: the reader lives the myth as a story at once true and unreal.

If one wishes to connect a mythical schema to a general history, to explain how it corresponds to the interests of a definite society, in short, to pass from semiology to ideology, it is obviously at the

[8] The freedom in choosing what one focuses on is a problem which does not belong to the province of semiology: it depends on the concrete situation of the subject.

[9] We receive the naming of the lion as a pure *example* of Latin grammar because we are, *as grown-ups*, in a creative position in relation to it. I shall come back later to the value of the context in this mythical schema.

level of the third type of focusing that one must place oneself: it is the reader of myths himself who must reveal their essential function. How does he receive this particular myth *today*? If he receives it in an innocent fashion, what is the point of proposing it to him? And if he reads it using his powers of reflection, like the mythologist, does it matter which alibi is presented? If the reader does not see French imperiality in the saluting Negro, it was not worth weighing the latter with it; and if he sees it, the myth is nothing more than a political proposition, honestly expressed. In one word, either the intention of the myth is too obscure to be efficacious, or it is too clear to be believed. In either case, where is the ambiguity?

This is but a false dilemma. Myth hides nothing and flaunts nothing: it distorts; myth is neither a lie nor a confession: it is an inflexion. Placed before the dilemma which I mentioned a moment ago, myth finds a third way out. Threatened with disappearance if it yields to either of the first two types of focusing, it gets out of this tight spot thanks to a compromise — it *is* this compromise. Entrusted with 'glossing over' an intentional concept, myth encounters nothing but betrayal in language, for language can only obliterate the concept if it hides it, or unmask it if it formulates it. The elaboration of a second-order semiological system will enable myth to escape this dilemma: driven to having either to unveil or to liquidate the concept, it will *naturalize* it.

We reach here the very principle of myth: it transforms history into nature. We now understand why, *in the eyes of the myth-consumer*, the intention, the adhomination of the concept can remain manifest without however appearing to have an interest in the matter: what causes mythical speech to be uttered is perfectly explicit, but it is immediately frozen into something natural; it is not read as a motive, but as a reason. If I read the Negro-saluting as symbol pure and simple of imperiality, I must renounce the reality of the picture, it discredits itself in my eyes when it becomes an instrument. Conversely, if I decipher the Negro's salute as an alibi of coloniality, I shatter the myth even more surely by the obviousness of its motivation. But for the myth-reader, the outcome is quite different: everything happens as if the picture *naturally* conjured up the concept, as if the signifier *gave a foundation* to the signified: the myth exists from the precise moment when French imperiality achieves the natural state: myth is speech justified *in excess*.

Here is a new example which will help understand clearly how the myth-reader is led to rationalize the signified by means of the signifier. We are in the month of July, I read a big headline in *France-Soir*: THE FALL IN PRICES: FIRST INDICATIONS. VEGETABLES: PRICE DROP BEGINS. Let us quickly sketch the semiological schema: the example being a sentence, the first system is purely linguistic. The signifier of the second system is composed here of a certain number of accidents, some lexical (the words: *first*, *begins*, *the* [fall]), some typographical (enormous headlines where the reader usually sees news of world importance). The signified or concept is what must be called by a barbarous but unavoidable neologism: *governmentality*, the Government presented by the national press as the Essence of efficacy. The signification of the myth follows clearly from this: fruit and vegetable prices are falling *because* the government has so decided. Now it so happens in this case (and this is on the whole fairly rare) that the newspaper itself has, two lines below, allowed one to see through the myth which it had just elaborated — whether this is due to self-assurance or honesty. It adds (in small type, it is true): 'The fall in prices is helped by the return of seasonal abundance.' This example is instructive for two reasons. Firstly it conspicuously shows that myth essentially aims at causing an immediate impression — it does not matter if one is later allowed to see through the myth, its action is assumed to be stronger than the rational explanations which may later belie it. This means that the reading of a myth is exhausted at one stroke. I cast a quick glance at my neighbour's *France-Soir*: I cull only a *meaning* there, but I read a true signification; I *receive* the presence of governmental action in the fall in fruit and vegetable prices. That is all, and that is enough. A more attentive reading of the myth will in no way increase its power or its ineffectiveness: a myth is at the same time imperfectible and unquestionable; time or knowledge will not make it better or worse.

Secondly, the naturalization of the concept, which I have just identified as the essential function of myth, is here exemplary. In a first (exclusively linguistic) system, causality would be, literally, natural: fruit and vegetable prices fall because they are in season. In the second (mythical) system, causality is artificial, false; but it creeps, so to speak, through the back door of Nature. This is why myth is experienced as innocent speech: not because its intentions are hidden—if they were hidden, they could not be efficacious—but because they are naturalized.

In fact, what allows the reader to consume myth innocently is that he does not see it as a semiological system but as an inductive one. Where there is only an equivalence, he sees a kind of causal process: the signifier and the signified have, in his eyes, a natural relationship. This confusion can be expressed otherwise: any semiological system is a system of values; now the myth-consumer takes the signification for a system of facts: myth is read as a factual system, whereas it is but a semiological system.

Myth as stolen language

What is characteristic of myth? To transform a meaning into form. In other words, myth is always a language-robbery. I rob the Negro who is saluting, the white and brown chalet, the seasonal fall in fruit prices, not to make them into examples or symbols, but to naturalize through them the Empire, my taste for Basque things, the Government. Are all primary languages a prey for myth? Is there no meaning which can resist this capture with which form threatens it? In fact, nothing can be safe from myth, myth can develop its second-order schema from any meaning and, as we saw, start from the very lack of meaning. But all languages do not resist equally well.

Articulated language, which is most often robbed by myth, offers little resistance. It contains in itself some mythical dispositions, the outline of a sign-structure meant to manifest the intention which led to its being used: it is what could be called the *expressiveness* of language. The imperative or the subjunctive mode, for instance, are the form of a particular signified, different from the meaning: the signified is here my will or my request. This is why some linguists have defined the indicative, for instance, as a zero state or degree, compared to the subjunctive or the imperative. Now in a fully constituted myth, the meaning is never at zero degree, and this is why the concept can distort it, naturalize it. We must remember once again that the privation of meaning is in no way a zero degree: this is why myth can perfectly well get hold of it, give it for instance the signification of the absurd, of surrealism, etc. At bottom, it would only be the zero degree which could resist myth.

Language lends itself to myth in another way: it is very rare that it imposes at the outset a full meaning which it is impossible to distort. This comes from the abstractness of its concept: the concept of *tree* is vague, it lends itself to multiple contingencies. True, a language always has at its disposal a whole appropriating organization (*this* tree, *the* tree *which*, etc.). But there always remains, around the final meaning, a halo of virtualities where other possible meanings are floating: the meaning can almost always be *interpreted*. One could say that a language offers to myth an open-work meaning. Myth can easily insinuate itself into it, and swell there: it is a robbery by colonization (for instance: *the* fall in prices has started. But what fall? That due to the season or that due to the government? the signification becomes here a parasite of the article, in spite of the latter being definite).

When the meaning is too full for myth to be able to invade it, myth goes around it, and carries it away bodily. This is what happens to mathematical language. In itself, it cannot be distorted, it has taken all possible precautions against *interpretation*: no parasitical signification can worm itself into it. And this is why, precisely, myth takes it away en bloc; it takes a certain mathematical formula ($E = mc^2$), and makes of this unalterable meaning the pure signifier of mathematicity. We can see that what is here robbed by myth is something which resists, something pure. Myth can reach everything, corrupt everything, and even the very act of refusing oneself to it. So that the more the language-object resists at first, the greater its final prostitution;

whoever here resists completely yields completely: Einstein on one side, *Paris-Match* on the other. One can give a temporal image of this conflict: mathematical language is a *finished* language, which derives its very perfection from this acceptance of death. Myth, on the contrary, is a language which does not want to die: it wrests from the meanings which give it its sustenance an insidious, degraded survival, it provokes in them an artificial reprieve in which it settles comfortably, it turns them into speaking corpses.

Here is another language which resists myth as much as it can: our poetic language. Contemporary poetry[10] is *a regressive semiological system*. Whereas myth aims at an ultra-signification, at the amplification of a first system, poetry, on the contrary, attempts to regain an infra-signification, a pre-semiological state of language; in short, it tries to transform the sign back into meaning: its ideal, ultimately, would be to reach not the meaning of words, but the meaning of things themselves.[11] This is why it clouds the language, increases as much as it can the abstractness of the concept and the arbitrariness of the sign and stretches to the limit the link between signifier and signified. The open-work structure of the concept is here maximally exploited: unlike what happens in prose, it is all the potential of the signified that the poetic sign tries to actualize, in the hope of at last reaching something like the transcendent quality of the thing, its natural (not human) meaning. Hence the essentialist ambitions of poetry, the conviction that it alone catches *the thing in itself*, inasmuch, precisely, as it wants to be an anti-language. All told, of all those who use speech, poets are the least formalist, for they are the

[10] Classical poetry, on the contrary, would be, according to such norms, a strongly mythical system, since it imposes on the meaning one extra signified, which is *regularity*. The alexandrine, for instance, has value both as meaning of a discourse and as signifier of a new whole, which is its poetic signification. Success, when it occurs, comes from the degree of apparent fusion of the two systems. It can be seen that we deal in no way with a harmony between content and form, but with an *elegant* absorption of one form into another. By *elegance* I mean the most economical use of the means employed. It is because of an age-old abuse that critics confuse *meaning* and *content*. The language is never anything but a system of forms, and the meaning is a form.

[11] We are again dealing here with the *meaning*, in Sartre's use of the term, as a natural quality of things, situated outside a semiological system (*Saint-Genet*, p. 283).

only ones who believe that the meaning of the words is only a form, with which they, being realists, cannot be content. This is why our modern poetry always asserts itself as a murder of language, a kind of spatial, tangible analogue of silence. Poetry occupies a position which is the reverse of that of myth: myth is a semiological system which has the pretension of transcending itself into a factual system; poetry is a semiological system which has the pretension of contracting into an essential system.

But here again, as in the case of mathematical language, the very resistance offered by poetry makes it an ideal prey for myth: the apparent lack of order of signs, which is the poetic facet of an essential order, is captured by myth, and transformed into an empty signifier, which will serve to *signify* poetry. This explains the *improbable* character of modern poetry: by fiercely refusing myth, poetry surrenders to it bound hand and foot. Conversely, the *rules* in classical poetry constituted an accepted myth, the conspicuous arbitrariness of which amounted to perfection of a kind, since the equilibrium of a semiological system comes from the arbitrariness of its signs.

A voluntary acceptance of myth can in fact define the whole of our traditional Literature. According to our norms, this Literature is an undoubted mythical system: there is a meaning, that of the discourse; there is a signifier, which is this same discourse as form or writing; there is a signified, which is the concept of literature; there is a signification, which is the literary discourse. I began to discuss this problem in *Writing Degree Zero*, which was, all told, nothing but a mythology of literary language. There I defined writing as the signifier of the literary myth, that is, as a form which is already filled with meaning and which receives from the concept of Literature a new signification.[12] I suggested

---

[12] *Style*, at least as I defined it then, is not a form, it does not belong to the province of a semiological analysis of Literature. In fact, style is a substance constantly threatened with formalization. To start with, it can perfectly well become degraded into a mode of writing: there is a 'Malraux-type' writing, and even in Malraux himself. Then, style can also become a particular language, that used by the writer *for himself and for himself alone*. Style then becomes a sort of solipsistic myth, the language which the writer speaks *to himself*. It is easy to understand that at such a degree of solidification, style calls for a deciphering. The works of J. P. Richard are an example of this necessary critique of styles.

that history, in modifying the writer's consciousness, had provoked, a hundred years or so ago, a moral crisis of literary language: writing was revealed as signifier, Literature as signification; rejecting the false nature of traditional literary language, the writer violently shifted his position in the direction of an anti-nature of language. The subversion of writing was the radical act by which a number of writers have attempted to reject Literature as a mythical system. Every revolt of this kind has been a murder of Literature as signification: all have postulated the reduction of literary discourse to a simple semiological system, or even, in the case of poetry, to a pre-semiological system. This is an immense task, which required radical types of behaviour: it is well known that some went as far as the pure and simple scuttling of the discourse, silence — whether real or transposed — appearing as the only possible weapon against the major power of myth: its recurrence.

It thus appears that it is extremely difficult to vanquish myth from the inside: for the very effort one makes in order to escape its stranglehold becomes in its turn the prey of myth: myth can always, as a last resort, signify the resistance which is brought to bear against it. Truth to tell, the best weapon against myth is perhaps to mythify it in its turn, and to produce an *artificial myth*: and this reconstituted myth will in fact be a mythology. Since myth robs language of something, why not rob myth? All that is needed is to use it as the departure point for a third semiological chain, to take its signification as the first term of a second myth. Literature offers some great examples of such artificial mythologies. I shall only evoke here Flaubert's *Bouvard and Pécuchet*. It is what could be called an experimental myth, a second-order myth. Bouvard and his friend Pécuchet represent a certain kind of bourgeoisie (which is incidentally in conflict with other bourgeois strata): their discourse *already* constitutes a mythical type of speech; its language does have a meaning, but this meaning is the empty form of a conceptual signified, which here is a kind of technological unsatedness. The meeting of meaning and concept forms, in this first mythical system, a signification which is the rhetoric of Bouvard and Pécuchet. It is at this point (I am breaking the process into its components for the sake of analysis) that Flaubert intervenes: to this first mythical system, which already is a second semiological system, he superimposes a third chain, in which the first link is the signification, or final term, of the first myth. The rhetoric of Bouvard and Pécuchet becomes the form of the new system; the concept here is due to Flaubert himself, to Flaubert's gaze on the myth which Bouvard and Pécuchet had built for themselves: it consists of their natively ineffectual inclinations, their inability to feel satisfied, the panic succession of their apprenticeships, in short what I would very much like to call (but I see storm-clouds on the horizon): bouvard-and-pécuchet-ity. As for the final signification, it is the book, it is *Bouvard and Pécuchet* for us. The power of the second myth is that it gives the first its basis as a naivety which is looked at. Flaubert has undertaken a real archaeological restoration of a given mythical speech: he is the Viollet-le-Duc of a certain bourgeois ideology. But less naive than Viollet-le-Duc, he has strewn his reconstitution with supplementary ornaments which demystify it. These ornaments (which are the form of the second myth) are subjunctive in kind: there is a semiological equivalence between the subjunctive restitution of the discourse of Bouvard and Pécuchet and their ineffectualness.[13]

Flaubert's great merit (and that of all artificial mythologies: there are remarkable ones in Sartre's work), is that he gave to the problem of realism a frankly semiological solution. True, it is a somewhat incomplete merit, for Flaubert's ideology, since the bourgeois was for him only an aesthetic eyesore, was not at all realistic. But at least he avoided the major sin in literary matters, which is to confuse ideological with semiological reality. As ideology, literary realism does not depend at all on the language spoken by the writer. Language is a form, it cannot possibly be either realistic or unrealistic. All it can do is either to be mythical or not, or perhaps, as in *Bouvard and Pécuchet*, counter-mythical. Now, unfortunately, there is no antipathy between realism and

---

[13] A subjunctive form because it is in the subjunctive mode that Latin expressed 'indirect style or discourse', which is an admirable instrument for demystification.

myth. It is well known how often our 'realistic' literature is mythical (if only as a crude myth of realism) and how our 'literature of the unreal' has at least the merit of being only slightly so. The wise thing would of course be to define the writer's realism as an essentially ideological problem. This certainly does not mean that there is no responsibility of form towards reality. But this responsibility can be measured only in semiological terms. A form can be judged (since forms are on trial) only as signification, not as expression. The writer's language is not expected to *represent* reality, but to signify it. This should impose on critics the duty of using two rigorously distinct methods: one must deal with the writer's realism either as an ideological substance (Marxist themes in Brecht's work, for instance) or as a semiological value (the props, the actors, the music, the colours in Brechtian dramaturgy). The ideal of course would be to combine these two types of criticism; the mistake which is constantly made is to confuse them: ideology has its methods, and so has semiology.

The bourgeoisie as a joint-stock company

Myth lends itself to history in two ways: by its form, which is only relatively motivated; by its concept, the nature of which is historical. One can therefore imagine a diachronic study of myths, whether one submits them to a retrospection (which means founding an historical mythology) or whether one follows some of yesterday's myths down to their present forms (which means founding prospective history). If I keep here to a synchronic sketch of contemporary myths, it is for an objective reason: our society is the privileged field of mythical significations. We must now say why.

Whatever the accidents, the compromises, the concessions and the political adventures, whatever the technical, economic, or even social changes which history brings us, our society is still a bourgeois society. I am not forgetting that since 1789, in France, several types of bourgeoisie have succeeded one another in power; but the same status—a certain regime of ownership, a certain order, a certain ideology – remains at a deeper level. Now a remarkable phenomenon occurs in the matter of naming this regime: as an economic fact, the bourgeoisie is *named* without any difficulty: capitalism is openly professed.[14] As a political fact, the bourgeoisie has some difficulty in acknowledging itself: there are no 'bourgeois' parties in the Chamber. As an ideological fact, it completely disappears: the bourgeoisie has obliterated its name in passing from reality to representation, from economic man to mental man. It comes to an agreement with the facts, but does not compromise about values, it makes its status undergo a real *ex-nominating* operation: the bourgeoisie is defined as *the social class which does not want to be named*. 'Bourgeois', 'petit-bourgeois', 'capitalism',[15] 'proletariat'[16] are the locus of an unceasing haemorrhage: meaning flows out of them until their very name becomes unnecessary.

This ex-nominating phenomenon is important; let us examine it a little more closely. Politically, the haemorrhage of the name 'bourgeois' is effected through the idea of *nation*. This was once a progressive idea, which has served to get rid of the aristocracy; today, the bourgeoisie merges into the nation, even if it has, in order to do so, to exclude from it the elements which it decides are allogenous (the Communists). This planned syncretism allows the bourgeoisie to attract the numerical support of its temporary allies, all the intermediate, therefore 'shapeless' classes. A long-continued use of the word *nation* has failed to depoliticize it in depth; the political substratum is there, very near the surface, and some circumstances make it suddenly manifest. There are in the Chamber some 'national' parties, and nominal syncretism here makes conspicuous what it had the ambition of hiding: an essential disparity. Thus the political vocabulary of the bourgeoisie already postulates that the universal

[14] 'The fate of capitalism is to make the worker wealthy,' *Paris-Match* tells us.

[15] The word 'capitalism' is taboo, not economically, but ideologically; it cannot possibly enter the vocabulary of bourgeois representations. Only in Farouk's Egypt could a prisoner be condemned by a tribunal for 'anti-capitalist plotting' in so many words.

[16] The bourgeoisie never uses the word 'Proletariat', which is supposed to be a Left-wing myth, except when it is in its interest to imagine the Proletariat being led astray by the Communist Party.

exists: for it, politics is already a representation, a fragment of ideology.

Politically, in spite of the universalistic effort of its vocabulary, the bourgeoisie eventually strikes against a resisting core which is, by definition, the revolutionary party. But this party can constitute only a political richness: in a bourgeois culture, there is neither proletarian culture nor proletarian morality, there is no proletarian art; ideologically, all that is rot bourgeois is obliged to *borrow* from the bourgeoisie. Bourgeois ideology can therefore spread over everything and in so doing lose its name without risk: no one here will throw this name of bourgeois back at it. It can without resistance subsume bourgeois theatre, art and humanity under their eternal analogues; in a word, it can ex-nominate itself without restraint when there is only one single human nature left: the defection from the name 'bourgeois' is here complete.

True, there are revolts against bourgeois ideology. This is what one generally calls the avant-garde. But these revolts are socially limited, they remain open to salvage. First, because they come from a small section of the bourgeoisie itself, from a minority group of artists and intellectuals, without public other than the class which they contest, and who remain dependent on its money in order to express themselves. Then, these revolts always get their inspiration from a very strongly made distinction between the ethically and the politically bourgeois: what the avant-garde contests is the bourgeois in art or morals—the shop-keeper, the Philistine, as in the heyday of Romanticism; but as for political contestation, there is none.[17] What the avant-garde does not tolerate about the bourgeoisie is its language, not its status. This does not necessarily mean that it approves of this status; simply, it leaves it aside. Whatever the violence of the

[17] It is remarkable that the adversaries of the bourgeoisie on matters of ethics or aesthetics remain for the most part indifferent, or even attached, to its political determinations. Conversely, its political adversaries neglect to issue a basic condemnation of its representations: they often go so far as to share them. This diversity of attacks benefits the bourgeoisie, it allows it to camouflage its name. For the bourgeoisie should be understood only as synthesis of its determinations and its representations.

provocation, the nature it finally endorses is that of 'derelict' man, not alienated man; and derelict man is still Eternal Man.[18]

This anonymity of the bourgeoisie becomes even more marked when one passes from bourgeois culture proper to its derived, vulgarized and applied forms, to what one could call public philosophy, that which sustains everyday life, civil ceremonials, secular rites, in short the unwritten norms of interrelationships in a bourgeois society. It is an illusion to reduce the dominant culture to its inventive core: there also is a bourgeois culture which consists of consumption alone. The whole of France is steeped in this anonymous ideology: our press, our films, our theatre, our pulp literature, our rituals, our Justice, our diplomacy, our conversations, our remarks about the weather, a murder trial, a touching wedding, the cooking we dream of, the garments we wear, everything, in everyday life, is dependent on the representation which the bourgeoisie *has and makes us have* of the relations between man and the world. These 'normalized' forms attract little attention, by the very fact of their extension, in which their origin is easily lost. They enjoy an intermediate position: being neither directly political nor directly ideological, they live peacefully between the action of the militants and the quarrels of the intellectuals; more or less abandoned by the former and the latter, they gravitate towards the enormous mass of the undifferentiated, of the insignificant, in short, of nature. Yet it is through its ethic that the bourgeoisie pervades France: practised on a national scale, bourgeois norms are experienced as the evident laws of a natural order—the further the bourgeois class propagates its representations, the more naturalized they become. The fact of the bourgeoisie becomes absorbed into an amorphous universe, whose sole inhabitant is Eternal Man, who is neither proletarian nor bourgeois.

It is therefore by penetrating the intermediate classes that the bourgeois ideology can most surely lose its name. Petit-bourgeois norms are the residue of bourgeois culture, they are bourgeois truths which have become degraded, impoverished, com-

---

[18] There can be figures of derelict man which lack all order (Ionesco for example). This does not affect in any way the security of the Essences.

mercialized, slightly archaic, or shall we say, out of date? The
political alliance of the bourgeoisie and the petite-bourgeoisie has
for more than a century determined the history of France; it has
rarely been broken, and each time only temporarily (1848, 1871,
1936). This alliance got closer as time passed, it gradually became
a symbiosis; transient awakenings might happen, but the common
ideology was never questioned again. The same 'natural' varnish
covers up all 'national' representations: the big wedding of the
bourgeoisie, which originates in a class ritual (the display and
consumption of wealth), can bear no relation to the economic
status of the lower middle-class: but through the press, the news,
and literature, it slowly becomes the very norm as dreamed,
though not actually lived, of the petit-bourgeois couple. The
bourgeoisie is constantly absorbing into its ideology a whole
section of humanity which does not have its basic status and
cannot live up to it except in imagination, that is, at the cost of an
immobilization and an impoverishment of consciousness.[19] By
spreading its representations over a whole catalogue of collective
images for petit-bourgeois use, the bourgeoisie countenances the
illusory lack of differentiation of the social classes: it is as from
the moment when a typist earning twenty pounds a month
recognizes herself in the big wedding of the bourgeoisie that
bourgeois ex-nomination achieves its full effect.

The flight from the name 'bourgeois' is not therefore an
illusory, accidental, secondary, natural or insignificant phenomenon: it is the bourgeois ideology itself, the process through
which the bourgeoisie transforms the reality of the world into an
image of the world, History into Nature. And this image has a
remarkable feature: it is upside down.[20] The status of the
bourgeoisie is particular, historical: man as represented by it
is universal, eternal. The bourgeois class has precisely built
its power on technical, scientific progress, on an unlimited

[19] To induce a collective content for the imagination is always an inhuman
undertaking, not only because dreaming essentializes life into destiny, but also
because dreams are impoverished, and the alibi of an absence.

[20] 'If men and their conditions appear throughout ideology inverted as in a
camera obscura, this phenomenon follows from their historical vital process ... '
(Marx, *The German Ideology*).

transformation of nature: bourgeois ideology yields in return an unchangeable nature. The first bourgeois philosophers pervaded the world with significations, subjected all things to an idea of the rational, and decreed that they were meant for man: bourgeois ideology is of the scientistic or the intuitive kind, it records facts or perceives values, but refuses explanations; the order of the world can be seen as sufficient or ineffable, it is never seen as significant. Finally, the basic idea of a perfectible mobile world, produces the inverted image of an unchanging humanity, characterized by an indefinite repetition of its identity. In a word, in the contemporary bourgeois society, the passage from the real to the ideological is defined as that from an *anti-physis* to a *pseudo-physis*.

Myth is depoliticized speech

And this is where we come back to myth. Semiology has taught us that myth has the task of giving an historical intention a natural justification, and making contingency appear eternal. Now this process is exactly that of bourgeois ideology. If our society is objectively the privileged field of mythical significations, it is because formally myth is the most appropriate instrument for the ideological inversion which defines this society: at all the levels of human communication, myth operates the inversion of *anti-physis* into *pseudo-physis*.

What the world supplies to myth is an historical reality, defined, even if this goes back quite a while, by the way in which men have produced or used it; and what myth gives in return is a *natural* image of this reality. And just as bourgeois ideology is defined by the abandonment of the name 'bourgeois', myth is constituted by the loss of the historical quality of things: in it, things lose the memory that they once were made. The world enters language as a dialectical relation between activities, between human actions; it comes out of myth as a harmonious display of essences. A conjuring trick has taken place; it has turned reality inside out, it has emptied it of history and has filled it with nature, it has removed from things their human meaning so as to make them signify a human insignificance. The function of myth is to empty reality: it is, literally, a ceaseless flowing out, a haemorrhage, or perhaps an evaporation, in short a perceptible absence.

It is now possible to complete the semiological definition of myth in a bourgeois society: *myth is depoliticized speech.* One must naturally understand *political* in its deeper meaning, as describing the whole of human relations in their real, social structure, in their power of making the world; one must above all give an active value to the prefix *de-*: here it represents an operational movement, it permanently embodies a defaulting. In the case of the soldier-Negro, for instance, what is got rid of is certainly not French imperiality (on the contrary, since what must be actualized is its presence); it is the contingent, historical, in one word: *fabricated*, quality of colonialism. Myth does not deny things, on the contrary, its function is to talk about them; simply, it purifies them, it makes them innocent, it gives them a natural and eternal justification, it gives them a clarity which is not that of an explanation but that of a statement of fact. If I *state the fact* of French imperiality without explaining it, I am very near to finding that it is natural and *goes without saying*: I am reassured. In passing from history to nature, myth acts economically: it abolishes the complexity of human acts, it gives them the simplicity of essences, it does away with all dialectics, with any going back beyond what is immediately visible, it organizes a world which is without contradictions because it is without depth, a world wide open and wallowing in the evident, it establishes a blissful clarity: things appear to mean something by themselves.[21]

However, is myth always depoliticized speech? In other words, is reality always political? Is it enough to speak about a thing naturally for it to become mythical? One could answer with Marx that the most natural object contains a political trace, however faint and diluted, the more or less memorable presence of the human act which has produced, fitted up, used, subjected or

[21] To the pleasure-principle of Freudian man could be added the clarity-principle of mythological humanity. All the ambiguity of myth is there: its clarity is euphoric.

rejected it.[22] The language-object, which '*speaks things*', can easily exhibit this trace; the metalanguage, which *speaks of things*, much less easily. Now myth always comes under the heading of metalanguage: the depoliticization which it carries out often supervenes against a background which is already naturalized, depoliticized by a general metalanguage which is trained to *celebrate* things, and no longer to '*act* them'. It goes without saying that the force needed by myth to distort its object is much less in the case of a tree than in the case of a Sudanese: in the latter case, the political load is very near the surface, a large quantity of artificial nature is needed in order to disperse it; in the former case, it is remote, purified by a whole century-old layer of metalanguage. There are, therefore, strong myths and weak myths; in the former, the political quantum is immediate, the depoliticization is abrupt; in the latter, the political quality of the object has *faded* like a colour, but the slightest thing can bring back its strength brutally: what is more *natural* than the sea? and what more 'political' than the sea celebrated by the makers of the film *The Lost Continent*?[23]

In fact, metalanguage constitutes a kind of preserve for myth. Men do not have with myth a relationship based on truth but on use: they depoliticize according to their needs. Some mythical objects are left dormant for a time; they are then no more than vague mythical schemata whose political load seems almost neutral. But this indicates only that their situation has brought this about, not that their structure is different. This is the case with our Latin-grammar example. We must note that here mythical speech works on a material which has long been transformed: the sentence by Aesop belongs to literature, it is at the very start mythified (therefore made innocent) by its being fiction. But it is enough to replace the initial term of the chain for an instant into its nature as language-object, to gauge the emptying of reality operated by myth: can one imagine the feelings of a *real* society of animals on finding itself transformed into a grammar example, into a predicative nature! In order to

[22] cf. Marx and the example of the cherry-tree, *The German Ideology*.
[23] cf. p. 94.

gauge the political load of an object and the mythical hollow which espouses it, one must never look at things from the point of view of the signification, but from that of the signifier, of the thing which has been robbed; and within the signifier, from the point of view of the language-object, that is, of the meaning. There is no doubt that if we consulted a *real* lion, he would maintain that the grammar example is a *strongly* depoliticized state, he would qualify as fully *political* the jurisprudence which leads him to claim a prey because he is the strongest, unless we deal with a bourgeois lion who would not fail to mythify his strength by giving it the form of a duty.

One can clearly see that in this case the political insignificance of the myth comes from its situation. Myth, as we know, is a value: it is enough to modify its circumstances, the general (and precarious) system in which it occurs, in order to regulate its scope with great accuracy. The field of the myth is in this case reduced to the second form of a French *lycée*. But I suppose that a child *enthralled* by the story of the lion, the heifer and the cow, and recovering through the life of the imagination the actual reality of these animals, would appreciate with much less unconcern than we do the disappearance of this lion changed into a predicate. In fact, we hold this myth to be politically insignificant only because it is not meant for us.

Myth on the Left

If myth is depoliticized speech, there is at least one type of speech which is the opposite of myth: that which *remains* political. Here we must go back to the distinction between language-object and metalanguage. If I am a woodcutter and I am led to name the tree which I am felling, whatever the form of my sentence, I 'speak the tree', I do not speak about it. This means that my language is operational, transitively linked to its object; between the tree and myself, there is nothing but my labour, that is to say, an action. This is a political language: it represents nature for me only inasmuch as I am going to transform it, it is a language thanks to which I '*act the object*'; the tree is not an image for me, it is simply the meaning of my action. But if I am not a woodcutter, I can no longer 'speak the tree', I can only speak *about* it, *on* it. My language is no longer the instrument of an 'acted-upon tree', it is the 'tree-celebrated' which becomes the instrument of my language. I no longer have anything more than an intransitive relationship with the tree; this tree is no longer the meaning of reality as a human action, it is an *image-at-one's-disposal*. Compared to the real language of the woodcutter, the language I create is a second-order language, a metalanguage in which I shall henceforth not 'act the things' but 'act their names', and which is to the primary language what the gesture is to the act. This second-order language is not entirely mythical, but it is the very locus where myth settles; for myth can work only on objects which have already received the mediation of a first language.

There is therefore one language which is not mythical, it is the language of man as a producer: wherever man speaks in order to transform reality and no longer to preserve it as an image, wherever he links his language to the making of things, meta-language is referred to a language-object, and myth is impossible. This is why revolutionary language proper cannot be mythical. Revolution is defined as a cathartic act meant to reveal the political load of the world: it *makes* the world; and its language, all of it, is functionally absorbed in this making. It is because it generates speech which is *fully*, that is to say initially and finally, political, and not, like myth, speech which is initially political and finally natural, that Revolution excludes myth. Just as bourgeois ex-nomination characterizes at once bourgeois ideology and myth itself, revolutionary denomination identifies revolution and the absence of myth. The bourgeoisie hides the fact that it is the bourgeoisie and thereby produces myth; revolution announces itself openly as revolution and thereby abolishes myth.

I have been asked whether there are myths 'on the Left'. Of course, inasmuch, precisely, as the Left is not revolution. Left-wing myth supervenes precisely at the moment when revolution changes itself into 'the Left', that is, when it accepts to wear a mask, to hide its name, to generate an innocent metalanguage and to distort itself into 'Nature'. This revolutionary ex-nomination may or may not be tactical, this is no place to discuss it. At any rate, it is sooner or later experienced as a process contrary to revolution, and it is always more or less in relation to myth that revolutionary history defines its 'deviations'. There came a day, for instance, when it was socialism itself which defined the Stalin myth. Stalin, as a spoken object, has exhibited for years, in their pure state, the constituent characters of mythical speech: a meaning, which was the real Stalin, that of history; a signifier, which was the ritual invocation to Stalin, and the *inevitable* character of the 'natural' epithets with which his name was surrounded; a signified, which was the intention to respect orthodoxy, discipline and unity, *appropriated* by the Communist parties to a definite situation; and a signification, which was a sanctified Stalin, whose historical determinants found themselves grounded in nature, sublimated under the name of Genius, that is, something irrational and inexpressible: here, depoliticization is evident, it fully reveals the presence of a myth.[24]

Yes, myth exists on the Left, but it does not at all have there the same qualities as bourgeois myth. *Left-wing myth is inessential.* To start with, the objects which it takes hold of are rare – only a few political notions – unless it has itself recourse to the whole repertoire of the bourgeois myths. Left-wing myth never reaches the immense field of human relationships, the very vast surface of 'insignificant' ideology. Everyday life is inaccessible to it: in a bourgeois society, there are no 'Left-wing' myths concerning marriage, cooking, the home, the theatre, the law, morality, etc. Then, it is an incidental myth, its use is not part of a strategy, as is the case with bourgeois myth, but only of a tactics, or, at the worst, of a deviation; if it occurs, it is as a myth suited to a convenience, not to a necessity.

Finally, and above all, this myth is, in essence, poverty-stricken. It does not know how to proliferate; being produced on order and for a temporally limited prospect, it is invented with

[24] It is remarkable that Krushchevism presented itself not as a political change, but essentially and only as a *linguistic conversion*. An incomplete conversion, incidentally, for Krushchev devalued Stalin, but did not explain him—did not re-politicize him.

difficulty. It lacks a major faculty, that of fabulizing. Whatever it does, there remains about it something stiff and literal, a suggestion of something done to order. As it is expressively put, it remains barren. In fact, what can be more meagre than the Stalin myth? No inventiveness here, and only a clumsy appropriation: the signifier of the myth (this form whose infinite wealth in bourgeois myth we have just seen) is not varied in the least: it is reduced to a litany.

This imperfection, if that is the word for it, comes from the nature of the 'Left': whatever the imprecision of the term, the Left always defines itself in relation to the oppressed, whether proletarian or colonized.[25] Now the speech of the oppressed can only be poor, monotonous, immediate: his destitution is the very yardstick of his language: he has only one, always the same, that of his actions; metalanguage is a luxury, he cannot yet have access to it. The speech of the oppressed is real, like that of the woodcutter; it is a transitive type of speech: it is quasi-unable to lie; lying is a richness, a lie presupposes property, truths and forms to spare. This essential barrenness produces rare, threadbare myths: either transient, or clumsily indiscreet; by their very being, they label themselves as myths, and point to their masks. And this mask is hardly that of a pseudo-physis: for that type of physis is also a richness of a sort, the oppressed can only borrow it: he is unable to throw out the real meaning of things, to give them the luxury of an empty form, open to the innocence of a false Nature. One can say that in a sense, Left-wing myth is always an artificial myth, a reconstituted myth: hence its clumsiness.

Myth on the Right

Statistically, myth is on the right. There, it is essential; well-fed, sleek, expansive, garrulous, it invents itself ceaselessly. It takes hold of everything, all aspects of the law, of morality, of aesthetics, of diplomacy, of household equipment, of Literature, of entertainment. Its expansion has the very dimensions of bourgeois

---

[25] Today it is the colonized peoples who assume to the full the ethical and political condition described by Marx as being that of the proletariat.

ex-nomination. The bourgeoisie wants to keep reality without keeping the appearances: it is therefore the very negativity of bourgeois appearance, infinite like every negativity, which solicits myth infinitely. The oppressed is nothing, he has only one language, that of his emancipation; the oppressor is everything, his language is rich, multiform, supple, with all the possible degrees of dignity at its disposal: he has an exclusive right to meta-language. The oppressed *makes* the world, he has only an active, transitive (political) language; the oppressor conserves it, his language is plenary, intransitive, gestural, theatrical: it is Myth. The language of the former aims at transforming, of the latter at eternalizing.

Does this completeness of the myths of Order (this is the name the bourgeoisie gives to itself) include inner differences? Are there, for instance, bourgeois myths and petit-bourgeois myths? There cannot be any fundamental differences, for whatever the public which consumes it, myth always postulated the immobility of Nature. But there can be degrees of fulfilment or expansion: some myths ripen better in some social strata: for myth also, there are micro-climates.

The myth of Childhood-as-Poet, for instance, is an *advanced* bourgeois myth: it has hardly come out of inventive culture (Cocteau, for example) and is just reaching consumer culture (*L'Express*). Part of the bourgeoisie can still find it too obviously invented, not mythical enough to feel entitled to countenance it (a whole part of bourgeois criticism works only with duly mythical materials). It is a myth which is not yet well run in, it does not yet contain enough *nature*: in order to make the Child-Poet part of a cosmogony, one must renounce the prodigy (Mozart, Rimbaud, etc.), and accept new norms, those of psycho-pedagogy, Freudianism, etc.: as a myth, it is still unripe.

Thus every myth can have its history and its geography; each is in fact the sign of the other: a myth ripens because it spreads. I have not been able to carry out any real study of the social geography of myths. But it is perfectly possible to draw what linguists would call the isoglosses of a myth, the lines which limit the social region where it is spoken. As this region is shifting, it would be better to speak of the waves of implantation of the myth. The Minou Drouet myth has thus had at least three waves of amplification: (1) *L'Express*; (2) *Paris-Match*, *Elle*; (3) *France-Soir*. Some myths hesitate: will they pass into tabloids, the home of the suburbanite of private means, the hairdresser's salon, the tube? The social geography of myths will remain difficult to trace as long as we lack an analytical sociology of the press.[26] But we can say that its place already exists.

Since we cannot yet draw up the list of the dialectal forms of bourgeois myth, we can always sketch its rhetorical forms. One must understand here by *rhetoric* a set of fixed, regulated, insistent figures, according to which the varied forms of the mythical signifier arrange themselves. These figures are transparent inasmuch as they do not affect the plasticity of the signifier; but they are already sufficiently conceptualized to adapt to an historical representation of the world (just as classical rhetoric can account for a representation of the Aristotelian type). It is through their rhetoric that bourgeois myths outline the general prospect of this *pseudo-physis* which defines the dream of the contemporary bourgeois world. Here are its principal figures:

1. *The inoculation.* I have already given examples of this very general figure, which consists in admitting the accidental evil of a class-bound institution the better to conceal its principial evil. One immunizes the contents of the collective imagination by means of a small inoculation of acknowledged evil; one thus protects it against the risk of a generalized subversion. This *liberal* treatment would not have been possible only a hundred years ago. Then, the bourgeois Good did not compromise with anything, it was quite stiff. It has become much more supple since: the bourgeoisie no longer hesitates to acknowledge some

[26] The circulation of newspapers is an insufficient datum. Other information comes only by accident. *Paris-Match* has given—significantly, as publicity—the composition of its public in terms of standard of living (*Le Figaro*, July 12th, 1955): out of each 100 readers living in town, 53 have a car, 49 a bathroom, etc., whereas the average standard of living in France is reckoned as follows: car, 22 per cent; bathroom, 13 per cent. That the purchasing power of the *Paris-Match* reader is high could have been predicted from the mythology of this publication.

localized subversions: the avant-garde, the irrational in child-hood, etc. It now lives in a balanced economy: as in any sound joint-stock company, the smaller shares—in law but not in fact—compensate the big ones.

2. *The privation of History.* Myth deprives the object of which it speaks of all History.[27] In it, history evaporates. It is a kind of ideal servant: it prepares all things, brings them, lays them out, the master arrives, it silently disappears: all that is left for one to do is to enjoy this beautiful object without wondering where it comes from. Or even better: it can only come from eternity: since the beginning of time, it has been made for bourgeois man, the Spain of the *Blue Guide* has been made for the tourist, and 'primitives' have prepared their dances with a view to an exotic festivity. We can see all the disturbing things which this felicitous figure removes from sight: both determinism and freedom. Nothing is produced, nothing is chosen: all one has to do is to possess these new objects from which all soiling trace of origin or choice has been removed. This miraculous evaporation of history is another form of a concept common to most bourgeois myths: the irresponsibility of man.

3. *Identification.* The petit-bourgeois is a man unable to imagine the Other.[28] If he comes face to face with him, he blinds himself, ignores and denies him, or else transforms him into himself. In the petit-bourgeois universe, all the experiences of confrontation are reverberating, any otherness is reduced to sameness. The spectacle or the tribunal, which are both places where the Other threatens to appear in full view, become mirrors. This is because the Other is a scandal which threatens his essence. Dominici cannot have access to social existence unless he is previously

[27] Marx: ' ... we must pay attention to this history, since ideology boils down to either an erroneous conception of this history, *or to a complete abstraction from it*' (*The German Ideology*).
[28] Marx: ' ... what makes them representative of the petit-bourgeois class, is that their minds, their consciousnesses do not extend beyond the limits which this class has set to its activities' (*The Eighteenth Brumaire*). And Gorki: 'the petit-bourgeois is the man who has preferred himself to all else.'

reduced to the state of a small simulacrum of the President of the Assizes or the Public Prosecutor: this is the price one must pay in order to condemn him justly, since Justice is a weighing operation and since scales can only weigh like against like. There are, in any petit-bourgeois consciousness, small simulacra of the hooligan, the parricide, the homosexual, etc., which periodically the judiciary extracts from its brain, puts in the dock, admonishes and condemns: one never tries anybody but analogues *who have gone astray*: it is a question of direction, not of nature, for *that's how men are*. Sometimes—rarely—the Other is revealed as irreducible: not because of a sudden scruple, but because *common sense* rebels: a man does not have a white skin, but a black one, another drinks pear juice, not *Pernod*. How can one assimilate the Negro, the Russian? There is here a figure for emergencies: exoticism. The Other becomes a pure object, a spectacle, a clown. Relegated to the confines of humanity, he no longer threatens the security of the home. This figure is chiefly petit-bourgeois. For, even if he is unable to experience the Other in himself, the bourgeois can at least imagine the place where he fits in: this is what is known as liberalism, which is a sort of intellectual equilibrium based on recognized places. The petit-bourgeois class is not liberal (it produces Fascism, whereas the bourgeoisie uses it): it follows the same route as the bourgeoisie, but lags behind.

4. *Tautology*. Yes, I know, it's an ugly word. But so is the thing. Tautology is this verbal device which consists in defining like by like (*'Drama is drama'*). We can view it as one of those types of magical behaviour dealt with by Sartre in his *Outline of a Theory of the Emotions*: one takes refuge in tautology as one does in fear, or anger, or sadness, when one is at a loss for an explanation: the accidental failure of language is magically identified with what one decides is a natural resistance of the object. In tautology, there is a double murder: one kills rationality because it resists one; one kills language because it betrays one. Tautology is a faint at the right moment, a saving aphasia, it is a death, or perhaps a comedy, the indignant 'representation' of the

rights of reality over and above language. Since it is magical, it can of course only take refuge behind the argument of authority: thus do parents at the end of their tether reply to the child who keeps on asking for explanations: *'because that's how it is'*, or even better: *'just because, that's all'* — a magical act ashamed of itself, which verbally makes the gesture of rationality, but immediately abandons the latter, and believes itself to be even with causality because it has uttered the word which introduces it. Tautology testifies to a profound distrust of language, which is rejected because it has failed. Now any refusal of language is a death. Tautology creates a dead, a motionless world.

5. *Neither-Norism*. By this I mean this mythological figure which consists in stating two opposites and balancing the one by the other so as to reject them both. (I want *neither* this *nor* that.) It is on the whole a bourgeois figure, for it relates to a modern form of liberalism. We find again here the figure of the scales: reality is first reduced to analogues; then it is weighed; finally, equality having been ascertained, it is got rid of. Here also there is magical behaviour: both parties are dismissed because it is embarrassing to choose between them; one flees from an intolerable reality, reducing it to two opposites which balance each other only inasmuch as they are purely formal, relieved of all their specific weight. Neither-Norism can have degraded forms: in astrology, for example, ill-luck is always followed by equal good-luck; they are always predicted in a prudently compensatory perspective: a final equilibrium immobilizes values, life, destiny, etc.: one no longer needs to choose, but only to endorse.

6. *The quantification of quality*. This is a figure which is latent in all the preceding ones. By reducing any quality to quantity, myth economizes intelligence: it understands reality more cheaply. I have given several examples of this mechanism which bourgeois — and especially petit-bourgeois — mythology does not hesitate to apply to aesthetic realities which it deems on the other hand to partake of an immaterial essence. Bourgeois

theatre is a good example of this contradiction: on the one hand, theatre is presented as an essence which cannot be reduced to any language and reveals itself only to the heart, to intuition. From this quality, it receives an irritable dignity (it is forbidden as a crime of 'lese-essence' to speak about the theatre *scientifically*: or rather, any intellectual way of viewing the theatre is discredited as scientism or pedantic language). On the other hand, bourgeois dramatic art rests on a pure quantification of effects: a whole circuit of computable appearances establishes a quantitative equality between the cost of a ticket and the tears of an actor or the luxuriousness of a set: what is currently meant by the 'naturalness' of an actor, for instance, is above all a conspicuous quantity of effects.

7. *The statement of fact.* Myths tend towards proverbs. Bourgeois ideology invests in this figure interests which are bound to its very essence: universalism, the refusal of any explanation, an unalterable hierarchy of the world. But we must again distinguish the language-object from the metalanguage. Popular, ancestral proverbs still partake of an instrumental grasp of the world as object. A rural statement of fact, such as '*the weather is fine*' keeps a real link with the usefulness of fine weather. It is an implicitly technological statement; the word, here, in spite of its general, abstract form, paves the way for actions, it inserts itself into a fabricating order: the farmer does not speak *about* the weather, he 'acts it', he draws it into his labour. All our popular proverbs thus represent active speech which has gradually solidified into reflexive speech, but where reflection is curtailed, reduced to a statement of fact, and so to speak timid, prudent, and closely hugging experience. Popular proverbs foresee more than they assert, they remain the speech of a humanity which is making itself, not one which is. Bourgeois aphorisms, on the other hand, belong to metalanguage; they are a second-order language which bears on objects already prepared. Their classical form is the maxim. Here the statement is no longer directed towards a world to be made; it must overlay one which is already made, bury the traces of this production under a self-evident

appearance of eternity: it is a counter-explanation, the decorous equivalent of a tautology, of this peremptory *because* which parents in need of knowledge hang above the heads of their children. The foundation of the bourgeois statement of fact is *common sense*, that is, truth when it stops on the arbitrary order of him who speaks it.

I have listed these rhetorical figures without any special order, and there may well be many others: some can become worn out, others can come into being. But it is obvious that those given here, such as they are, fall into two great categories, which are like the Zodiacal Signs of the bourgeois universe: the Essences and the Scales. Bourgeois ideology continuously transforms the products of history into essential types. Just as the cuttlefish squirts its ink in order to protect itself, it cannot rest until it has obscured the ceaseless making of the world, fixated this world into an object which can be for ever possessed, catalogued its riches, embalmed it, and injected into reality some purifying essence which will stop its transformation, its flight towards other forms of existence. And these riches, thus fixated and frozen, will at last become computable: bourgeois morality will essentially be a weighing operation, the essences will be placed in scales of which bourgeois man will remain the motionless beam. For the very end of myths is to immobilize the world: they must suggest and mimic a universal order which has fixated once and for all the hierarchy of possessions. Thus, every day and everywhere, man is stopped by myths, referred by them to this motionless prototype which lives in his place, stifles him in the manner of a huge internal parasite and assigns to his activity the narrow limits within which he is allowed to suffer without upsetting the world: bourgeois pseudo-physis is in the fullest sense a prohibition for man against inventing himself. Myths are nothing but this ceaseless, untiring solicitation, this insidious and inflexible demand that all men recognize themselves in this image, eternal yet bearing a date, which was built of them one day as if for all time. For the Nature, in which they are locked up under the pretext of being eternalized, is nothing but an Usage. And it is this Usage, however lofty, that they must take in hand and transform.

Necessity and limits of mythology

I must, as a conclusion, say a few words about the mythologist himself. This term is rather grand and self-assured. Yet one can predict for the mythologist, if there ever is one, a few difficulties, in feeling if not in method. True, he will have no trouble in feeling justified: whatever its mistakes, mythology is certain to participate in the making of the world. Holding as a principle that man in a bourgeois society is at every turn plunged into a false Nature, it attempts to find again under the assumed innocence of the most unsophisticated relationships, the profound alienation which this innocence is meant to make one accept. The unveiling which it carries out is therefore a political act: founded on a responsible idea of language, mythology thereby postulates the freedom of the latter. It is certain that in this sense mythology *harmonizes* with the world, not as it is, but as it wants to create itself (Brecht had for this an efficiently ambiguous word: *Einverstandnis*, at once an understanding of reality and a complicity with it).

This harmony justifies the mythologist but does not fulfil him: his status still remains basically one of being excluded. Justified by the political dimension, the mythologist is still at a distance from it. His speech is a metalanguage, it 'acts' nothing; at the most, it unveils—or does it? To whom? His task always remains ambiguous, hampered by its ethical origin. He can live revolutionary action only vicariously: hence the self-conscious character of his function, this something a little stiff and painstaking, muddled and excessively simplified which brands any intellectual behaviour with an openly political foundation ('uncommitted' types of literature are infinitely more 'elegant'; they are in their place in metalanguage).

Also, the mythologist cuts himself off from all the myth-consumers, and this is no small matter. If this applied to a particular section of the collectivity, well and good.[29] But when a myth reaches the entire community, it is from the latter that the mythologist must become estranged if he wants to liberate the myth. Any myth with some degree of generality is in fact ambiguous, because it represents the very humanity of those who, having nothing, have borrowed it. To decipher the Tour de France or the 'good French Wine' is to cut oneself off from those who are entertained or warmed up by them. The mythologist is condemned to live in a theoretical sociality; for him, to be in society is, at best, to be truthful: his utmost sociality dwells in his utmost morality. His connection with the world is of the order of sarcasm.

One must even go further: in a sense, the mythologist is excluded from this history in the name of which he professes to act. The havoc which he wreaks in the language of the community is absolute for him, it fills his assignment to the brim: he must live this assignment without any hope of going back or any assumption of payment. It is forbidden for him to imagine what the world will concretely be like, when the immediate object of his criticism has disappeared. Utopia is an impossible luxury for him: he greatly doubts that tomorrow's truths will be the exact reverse of today's lies. History never ensures the triumph pure and simple of something over its opposite: it unveils, while making itself, unimaginable solutions, unforeseeable syntheses. The mythologist is not even in a Moses-like situation: he cannot see the Promised Land. For him, tomorrow's positivity is entirely hidden by today's negativity. All the values of his undertaking appear to him as acts of destruction: the latter accurately cover the former, nothing protrudes. This subjective grasp of history in which the potent seed of the future *is nothing but* the most profound apocalypse of the present has been expressed by Saint-Just in a strange saying: '*What constitutes the*

---

[29] It is not only from the public that one becomes estranged; it is sometimes also from the very object of the myth. In order to demystify Poetic Childhood, for instance, I have had, so to speak, *to lack confidence* in Minou Drouet the child. I have had to ignore, in her, under the enormous myth with which she is cumbered, something like a tender, open, possibility. It is never a good thing to speak *against* a little girl.

Republic is the total destruction of what is opposed to it.' This must not, I think, be understood in the trivial sense of: 'One has to clear the way before reconstructing.' The copula has an exhaustive meaning: there is for some men a subjective dark night of history where the future becomes an essence, the essential destruction of the past.

One last exclusion threatens the mythologist: he constantly runs the risk of causing the reality which he purports to protect, to disappear. Quite apart from all speech, the *D.S. 19* is a technologically defined object: it is capable of a certain speed, it meets the wind in a certain way, etc. And this type of reality cannot be spoken of by the mythologist. The mechanic, the engineer, even the user, '*speak* the object'; but the mythologist is condemned to metalanguage. This exclusion already has a name: it is what is called ideologism. Zhdanovism has roundly condemned it (without proving, incidentally, that it was, *for the time being*, avoidable) in the early Lukàcs, in Marr's linguistics, in works like those of Bénichou or Goldmann, opposing to it the reticence of a reality inaccessible to ideology, such as that of language according to Stalin. It is true that ideologism resolves the contradiction of alienated reality by an amputation, not a synthesis (but as for Zhdanovism, it does not even resolve it): wine is objectively good, and *at the same time*, the goodness of wine is a myth: here is the aporia. The mythologist gets out of this as best he can: he deals with the goodness of wine, not with the wine itself, just as the historian deals with Pascal's ideology, not with the *Pensées* in themselves.[30]

It seems that this is a difficulty pertaining to our times: there is as yet only one possible choice, and this choice can bear only on two equally extreme methods: either to posit a reality which is entirely permeable to history, and ideologize; or, conversely, to posit a reality which is *ultimately* impenetrable, irreducible, and, in this case, poetize. In a word, I do not yet see a synthesis

[30] Even here, in these mythologies, I have used trickery: finding it painful constantly to work on the evaporation of reality, I have started to make it excessively dense, and to discover in it a surprising compactness which I savoured with delight, and I have given a few examples of 'substantial psycho-analysis' about some mythical objects.

between ideology and poetry (by poetry I understand, in a very general way, the search for the inalienable meaning of things).

The fact that we cannot manage to achieve more than an unstable grasp of reality doubtless gives the measure of our present alienation: we constantly drift between the object and its demystification, powerless to render its wholeness. For if we penetrate the object, we liberate it but we destroy it; and if we acknowledge its full weight, we respect it, but we restore it to a state which is still mystified. It would seem that we are condemned for some time yet always to speak *excessively* about reality. This is probably because ideologism and its opposite are types of behaviour which are still magical, terrorized, blinded and fascinated by the split in the social world. And yet, this is what we must seek: a reconciliation between reality and men, between description and explanation, between object and knowledge.